PARENTING

...WITH A

Twist

Dear Tracy, Pheonix & Sophia,

Cheers to an awesome parenting experience!

A.H.Hepburn

Publication data:

Author: Scotchburn, Amber

Editing: Sylvia Taylor
Book design: Peggy Richardson
Logo and "wheel" design: Amanda Sears of Studio S., New Zealand
Additional Graphics: iStock.com and all-free-download.com

Title: Parenting with a twist / Amber Scotchburn.

Categories: 1. Parenting. 2. Family. I. Title.

ISBN 978-0-9952804-3-4 (softcover)

Tutoring With a Twist, Publisher

Book Sales in North America & Internationally:

Order Online at: parentingwithatwist.com

Printed in the USA.

Amber Scotchburn BSW BEd

Part of the *Success...With A Twist* Series

Acknowledgements

I would like to thank the following people who have shaped who I am today! My fantastical children — there is no way I could have written this book without their daily influence; my parents, Rosemary & Tom, — for being my first fantastical role models; Aunt Nancy — for being my childhood idol and for shaping my career path which heavily influences how I parent; Mary Millard — for showing me the importance of family and teaching me your family traditions; Mary Wragg Morris — for treating me just like a daughter; Mrs. Walker — for giving me roots and love in what was a very turbulent time in my life; Aunt Ruthie — for embodying what I want my relationship to always be like with my children; my former students, Donna — for the honour of asking me to be her daughter's godmother and Jenn — for being there for my kids and I in my weakest hour; Trish/Rudi — for opening their home and hearts to me when we were new to the Island; my partner, Mike — for being a role model of quality parenting and for being my biggest cheerleader; Joe — for the unconditional support and love he gives to all; Gina — for believing in my author abilities which put me on this track; Colin — for seeing the potential in me and my business; Monique — for opening my eyes to my sacred gift of writing; Peggy — for finding the magical words that got me to write this book; Sylvia — for helping to make this the best parenting book ever! And, to the countless parents that have trusted me with their children and allowed me into their worlds for the past two decades — I am forever grateful, as with every encounter I grow more as a parent.

"Making the decision to have a child - it is momentous. It is to decide forever to have your heart go walking around outside your body."

- Elizabeth Stone

Parenting…With A Twist is dedicated to my children, River and Marley.

$\mathcal{T}$able of Contents

Parenting Tip #8

Parenting Tip #9

Parenting Tip #10   127

"I didn't have the gift of Amber's guidance... But you do, and I implore you to make use of it."

- Debra Poneman

Foreword

From Debra Poneman

Bestselling Author, Founder of "Yes to Success" and Co-Founder of "Your Year of Miracles"

In 1988 I was at the top of my game. My success seminar company had reps teaching on four continents, I was about to sign a contract for my own daytime TV talk show, my book was in the hands of a top New York publisher and I had more requests for speaking engagements than I had space on my calendar.

But I taught that the only way to live real and lasting success was to follow your heart.

So true to my teaching, one fateful day I simply gave it all up—every bit of it—the seminars, the speaking, the book. That day was the day when I first felt this little being that was growing inside of me madly kicking away and I saw the outline of her tiny foot pushing on my hugely rounded belly.

My heart knew that it did not want to be followed anywhere outside the energy field of this amazing creature.

And in my naiveté, I actually believed that the orderliness in my life now filled with meetings and deadlines, interviews and appointments was going to continue with the clockwork precision I was used to. I was simply transitioning to a new career. And it did continue— until the day my daughter was born.

About 10 hours into my perfect labor, taking place in the sweet and serene atmosphere of my clean and well-appointed bedroom, it was discovered that I had cephalopelvic disproportion. That baby's very large head was not going to fit through this mama's very small pelvis.

Before you could say, "I should have had an ultrasound," I endured a harrowing transfer to the local emergency room, a life-saving C-section, the discovery of organ damage, 24 hours in intensive care and a six-day stay at the local hospital with my bundle of joy glued to my side. She looked so innocent.

Thus my journey into the wildly chaotic, often exhausting, frequently heart-rending, sometimes merciless, and always unpredictable world of motherhood began with a bang.

Hundreds of sleepless nights, three rounds of mastitis, four questionable babysitters and thousands of diapers later - biodegradable, organic, of course - I remember my feeling of helplessness as Deanna had a major meltdown at the local grocery store and thinking, "I know now why they say, 'I wish she came with a handbook.'"

I had known what to expect when I was expecting, but that was the easy part. Now with my daughter wailing with such determination that I was sure security was going to come and cart me away to children's services, I seriously wished that someone would have written a book to guide me through the rest of this perilous expedition called motherhood—after the "expecting" part.

That wish only became more fervent as the years went on and I wondered if it was indulgent that our bedroom, once a haven of peace and serenity, was really the ideal spot for the large wooden jungle gym it now sported…and more fervent yet as I agonized over whether my five-year-old should really continue to play soccer when it was below freezing with the wind chill, and all she did anyway was stand and look at the sky while twirling her hair around her little finger.

And as Deanna got older, I had no idea how much pressure I should apply for her to excel in school or how much I should interfere when she stepped on her baby brother. Should I defend the teacher and instill respect for authority when there was a conflict—even when I knew that she was right?

And what should I do about my son who has a genius IQ and absolutely no interest whatsoever in traditional learning? And how many times should I drive to school to bring him the lunch he forgot even though I had handed it to him one minute before he walked out the door?

How could I know what was an appropriate level of discipline and what do I do if the behavior that warrants discipline is something they modeled from me or my husband?

And when they were teens, I never knew how much I should be listening and how much I should be talking. Wasn't I the one that was supposed to have the answers?

In other words, where was Amber Scotchburn when I needed her?

I didn't have the gift of Amber's guidance as I slogged through what I mistakenly thought was going to be all about delightful Mommy and Me playgroups and fun family trips to Disneyland. But you do have her guidance—and I implore you to make use of it.

With insight, clarity and the authority that comes from sixteen years as a parent and two decades as an educator, Amber provides us with the definitive guide to creative parenting that will result in an ever growing understanding and love for your child, and the type of mutual respect that fosters a strong lifelong bond.

This book was created as a user-friendly manual. It's not something you read once and stick on a shelf until you're ready to give it to the library fund-raiser. Instead it will be your companion throughout your child's life, giving you the answers you need when you need them or guiding you how to discover your own.

In *Parenting….With a Twist*, Amber asks us what are our wishes, dreams and hopes as parents and then as she leads us through parent-land she shows us that unconditional acceptance and loving your children for who they are will allow those dreams to come true.

Amber is brilliant, astute, insightful, thorough, and most of all, she walks her talk. She is the teacher who lives her teachings. Her children are fortunate to have her as their mom, and we are beyond fortunate to have her, and *Parenting…With a Twist*, as a trusted guide throughout this great adventure we call Parenthood.

"... Let's discover the magic in getting to know your child, and fall back in love with them at every age."

- Amber Scotchburn

Congratulations!

You have taken the first step to mastering your family's happiness and success by simply committing to reading this book. You are well on your way to creating confident, resilient, and empowered children who are prepared to deal with whatever life brings them by being success-ready. By success-ready we mean that your children will be hopeful, engaged, thriving, self-sufficient, and prosperous. Through reading this book and doing our hands-on activities, you will become the parent you've always wanted to be.

Why do we want our children to be success-ready? Because being success-ready is significantly related to school performance—influencing outcomes such as grades, credits earned, achievement scores, likelihood to stay in school, and future employment. Research shows that people are best prepared for the rigors of life when they have high hopes for the future, are deeply involved in and enthusiastic about school, and feel emotionally and physically well enough to take advantage of learning opportunities.

Do you sometimes feel like you don't want 'to parent,' you'd rather curl up on the couch and simply zone out? But then you realize that you have two eyes starring at you, depending on you to feed them, clothe them, give them love, make them feel safe, help them with their homework, remind them that they should brush their teeth and the endless, exhausting list goes on! While children don't come with an instruction booklet, we've created this book as a manual to help you 'to parent.'

I'd also like to thank you on behalf of your child and all whom they will encounter in their lives. You are doing something to ensure their success! Also, remember this is just a moment in time. By doing something about it, you are consciously aiding them to form habits and behaviours that are going to be life altering. Enjoy this moment in time and know that you are making a difference.

We understand that there is a lot of intense pressure on parents to produce a successful child, teenager and young adult. Often this pressure starts from even the mere thought of having a child. Let us walk you through this journey and relieve some of your pressure.

As a social worker, teacher, tutoring agency CEO, bestselling author, and nationally sought-after parenting expert, I'm here to help YOU be the parent you've always wanted to be.

As an everyday parent, you will be able to do your own Parenting Skills Assessment through reading this book. And then, place your trust in our Signature *Success… With A Twist* system to help you transform the knowledge gleaned from this skills assessment and from the 'hands-on' and 'interactive' experiences found throughout the book to empower you to discover the positive parent within.

Instead of using punitive measures as your first line of discipline, let's discover the magic in getting to know your child and fall back in love with them at every age. Let's learn why it's important for your child to say "no" and even lie to you. Let's explore not allowing school grades to define your child. Let's understand all of your child's behaviours, especially the ones that drive you the most insane.

Predictors of Success

The Scary Statistics

Let's begin by highlighting some recent statistics that reveal that we are not raising success-ready children. We've included statistics from school and home life. If anybody questions why you are reading this book, just share a scary stat with them.

In relation to school, for students between Grades 5-12, did you know that:

- Only 1 in 3 students feel they are success-ready.

- Almost 50% of students lack hope for the future, reporting they feel stuck in their lives or discouraged about the future.

- Almost 50% of students are disengaged with school, reporting they feel not engaged or are actively disengaged.

- Almost 70% of students do not receive financial literacy information at school.

In relation to home life, did you know that:

- Only 1% of parents ensure their children save anything from their allowance.

- Mother's stress gives rise to lower math skills. Spending quality time with a teenager gives rise to higher math skills.

- The number of hours that moms spend with kids between ages 3 and 11 does little to predict the child's behaviour, well-being, or achievement. But stress, income, and quality interactions do.

- Almost 60% of young adults, referred to as the 'boomerang generation'—those between the ages of twenty to thirty-four—live in their childhood bedrooms and basements in alarmingly high numbers. And that 42% of these parents don't charge rent in these situations; while 80% of these parents still buy groceries and do the cooking.

By encouraging all three predictors of success—hope, engagement, and wellbeing—families can help their children become success-ready. And, if you don't want your children living at home until they are thirty-four, I invite you to read on. (Yes, thirty-four years of age. As we have four children, you can be darn sure that this statistic won't be coming true in our home.)

What We Know To Be True

• Engaged students are more likely to have strong relationships and feel they have opportunities.

• Hopeful students are more engaged in life and more likely to believe in success after graduation.

And while there isn't a set recipe for raising successful children, psychological research has pointed to a handful of factors that predict success. Guess what? You are your children's best role model. Think back: how 'success-ready' were you when you left school and home? And, let's be honest with ourselves, how 'success-ready' are you now?

Impossible To I'm Possible

In order to assist families, we've identified the Top Positive Parenting Tips that parents need in order to raise confident, resilient and empowered children. We are presenting some painful truths but we are also going to provide you with some insights into how you can begin to correct these parenting failures. (And you will learn that we don't think of failure as a bad word and would actually like you to fail early and fail often!)

Throughout the workbook you will see different icons—stop and reflect on what we are asking you to do. See where you can begin to make changes today that will immediately correct the toxic behaviours you may be currently engaging in.

Both your parenting and your life will flourish, as this book will basically be your toolbox of parenting. You will get to assess how you are acting, thinking, behaving and being, right now as a parent! And decide; are these things you want to continue doing? Are there things you would like to change or shift?

If you've thought it was impossible to be the parent you want to be, I'm inviting you right now to change IMPOSSIBLE into "I'M POSSIBLE!" You can be that parent you've always wanted to be.

A good friend told me, when I was pregnant with my first child, that it's not how much you save for your children for their first car, house, marriage, schooling, or whatever you deem as important—it's how much you save for them for counselling, because no matter what you do as a parent, you somehow mess it up. I invite you to approach reading this book knowing that it will help you to mess up a little bit less! You've done your best up to now and you are going to do better, as you will now know better.

Today marks the start of your Successful Parenthood Journey—I'm excited for you!

"Be who are you meant to be, instead of who you think you should be, what you think you can't be, or living where you got stuck. YOU get to choose your parenting path."

- Amber Scotchburn

How To Read This Book

Do you have a favourite family recipe card that looks scruffy and has food stains on it from it being so well-used? That is how I want you to treat this book. So fold the corners, keep it accessible for use, write all over it, and get stains on it. I want this book to be as well-loved and used as that recipe card.

There is a Japanese word, tsundoku, which means buying books and letting them pile up unread. Please don't tsundoku this book—it's not meant to be 'shelf help.' (You've already learned something new but that doesn't mean you can already put the book down.)

Guidelines

Follow these guidelines when reading the book to make sure you get the most out of the experience. I 'pinky-promise' you that by using the knowledge in this book as a guide and through doing the exercises that accompany it, you will transform your parenting world.

- Do your best to schedule some uninterrupted time. If this isn't doable for you, do it while your child is doing homework or is doing their daily reading. (Yes, your child needs to be reading every day. Anything—even if it's just the cereal box.) Scheduling is important, just as you'd schedule a doctor's appointment or an activity for your child, to ensure it gets done.

- Be aware of what point in the day is best for you to read and schedule time to read then.

- Get comfortable. Get yourself a beverage or a snack. Snuggle under a blanket. Go out into nature. Hang out in your favourite coffee place. Find your happy reading space!

- Gather the tools that will help you retain information and things that resonate with you: a highlighter, writing material like a pen or pencil, paper, stickies to make notes in the margin and/or a notebook to record your thoughts.

- Please make a note of how to connect with us, as there are key moments in the book where we suggest that reaching out to us is imperative to your growth.

- Choose an Accountability Partner. This is an ally who helps you work toward your goals. Someone who is encouraging, compassionate, emotionally resilient, willing to give constructive feedback and see the greatness in you. You can connect regularly in person, by phone or Skype or even emails. If you don't have someone like this in your life, connect with us and we will do our best to find you one through our Parenting… With A Twist community.

- I invite you to use your agenda to write down when you began the book and when you plan to finish it. In making this plan, you will need to take into account the time it will take to read the chapter as well as do the reflection questions at the end of each chapter. Other common words for agendas are calendars, planners, and day-timers. This tool will play a key role in this journey so ensure you have one!

- Next, I'd like you to share this plan with your Accountability Partner. Invite them to go on this journey with you! It's okay if you have to adjust your timeline, just be honest with yourself about it. Share your targeted deadline with us.

- Write down any questions you may have as you go through this book and connect with us to have them answered.

- For those readers that would like more of a hands-on approach through this journey, connect with us to learn more about our *Parenting… With A Twist Workbook* and video series. The *Parenting… With A Twist Workbook* contains the Parenting Skills Questions found in this book. The bonus is that the Workbook gives more of an in-depth look into why we are asking those questions and what you can do if you get stuck, as well as the physical space to write the answers down. We know this journey can be tough and we also know it's one of the most important ones you will ever take, so we created the *Parenting… With A Twist Video Series* to offer the option to be coached through this journey by one of our team members.

We are invested in your success, so please remember to connect with
us if you run into any difficulties or need any help with these questions.

You can connect with us at our *Parenting… With A Twist*
Facebook page at Facebook.com/parentingwithatwist,
or click to parentingwithatwist.com

Our Success... With A Twist System

Our Signature Success System has been helping families for over two decades reach their chosen accomplishments. It's the foundation of the work we've done with students, teachers, parents, families, community agencies and individuals. For the first time in print, we are sharing this system with you. The best aspect of this process is that it's repeatable to any area of your life, once you understand it. It's based on having a goal or something you want to change in your life and the mindset and actions you need to reach that.

You will see these different icons throughout the book that represent a mindset that we, at Parenting…With A Twist, would like you to start being conscious of. These icons make up our Signature Success System that will help you on your parenting success journey. Spend some time studying and reflecting upon each icon's meaning and remember that when you get to that icon in the book, you can always flip back to this page to remember the deeper meaning behind them. Also remember, once you master this process for your parenting goal, you can use the same steps to work on other areas of your life that you'd like to change!

Star: Hopes, Wishes, Dreams & Desires

Think of your dreams, goals, wishes, hopes and desires as represented by stars. Our journey together will be to help you reach those stars.

Any time you start to feel discouraged as you read through the book or if you have a particularly challenging parenting moment, this image will remind you that you can reach your stars.

Circles: Different Lenses We Put On

When you see the icon above, we are inviting you to become aware of the perspective you see the world through and to question thoughts and patterns that could prevent you from reaching your life dreams. Yes, you can be the parent you've always wanted to be.

As you encountered different experiences through your life, (see the Heart icon below) you formed different ways of being in the world. These ways influence how you see the world. The lens icon represents what particular lens you are 'looking through' in various experiences.

Staying calm in a parenting situation versus losing it in a parenting situation, will all depend on what lens you are looking through. This is why parents can have completely different reactions to the same behaviours in their child. And think of the times when you don't even truly understand why you've lost it; you are simply reacting based on your lens.

I invite you to start being aware of the lenses you wear that cause you to act, think and feel the way you do. The way in which this book is written will give you the guidance to start reflecting upon which lens you are wearing. We want you to be aware that you can choose which lens to put on.

For instance, it's very damaging to respond to situations with the word "can't." Some examples of this are: "We can't afford that." "I can't be the parent I've always wanted to be." Start to catch yourself when you are using that word as it shuts down other possibilities. When it's an automatic response, you are still seeing the world through an old lens.

How can you replace automatically using the word "can't" in your sentences? Recognize that it's a choice to do or not to do something in this moment, but that is different than saying: "I can't do it." And if you want to do it but are feeling you have to make a different choice, examine why. Are there circumstances you can affect change in? If so, why not strive towards making those changes. If, right now, it is something that is beyond your control, still make note of it. You never know, once you've acknowledged something, what opportunity might present itself.

Another word to be aware of is 'should.' When it feels like you 'should' be doing an action, examine this feeling. Are you making a conscious choice to do whatever the action is? Or is there an emotion driving you to doing this action? "I should call that person back." "I should really make a healthy dinner tonight." Be mindful of how many shoulds you are thinking in relation to parenting as this will gauge how consciously you are parenting.

When we frame our thoughts using the words can't and should, we are giving our power away. It's much more powerful to make a conscious choice to do something or not do it.

 Clapperboard: Miss Take versus Mistake
& A.C.T. (Action Changes Things)
Shift your mindset to change the spelling of "mistake" to "miss take" so that you can live without fear of making an error. Embracing each moment that life offers to love, to learn, and to be grateful. Yes, you've not messed up your kids…yet!

When you see a clapperboard, it reminds you to replace "mistake" with "miss take." In movie making there are a million miss takes along the way to the big screen, to get it just right. Directors adjust the lighting, the music, the script, the costumes, the setting, etc. for the take to be exactly the way they want it. Along the parenting path with your child, you will make miss takes, but your child and you are worth all the takes it takes to get it right. Imagine yelling, "Plot Twist" in your head when things aren't going exactly as planned. Or, imagine the clapperboard giving you another opportunity to get it right. We will help you make the adjustments you need to direct your parenting life as you want it to be!

View miss takes as what your imagination creates as opposed to what is actually happening. When a child is learning to walk and they fall, our lens may tell us that something went wrong. However, what we know to be true is that anybody who is just learning to walk is going to fall as part of their natural progression to actually walking. Therefore, seeing the act of falling like a mistake, is really our perception of something gone wrong as opposed to what actually is. If you look at the act of falling like a miss take, all that happened is that they fell and next time would do something different to not fall. When your child is learning to walk, you expect failure to happen. So why not expect failure in other aspects of your child's life, as well as your own life? Be cautious if you think of failure as something negative instead of something that is necessary on the path to success.

Let's think about the terms used in the making of a movie, like, "Act 1, Scene 1." Now think of the acronym A.C.T. meaning, Action Changes Things. As you make your miss takes, you will need to take action in order to make the necessary changes. These actions will tweak something in order to get you closer to where you want to be because…A.C.T.

Heart: Life Experiences that Shape Us

When you see the heart icon, realize that while it's our heart that keeps us alive, it also holds a collection of everything that has happened to us in our life and what shapes us into who we are today. It's important to note that not all the events that have shaped us are happy ones. If we hold on to our life events and let them dictate how we move forward in life, we aren't living consciously and we aren't going to be able to make significant changes.

Separate yourself from your 'story.' Be who are you meant to be, instead of who you think you should be, what you think you can't be, or living where you got stuck. YOU get to choose your parenting path.

The heart questions are specifically designed to bring you to living in the present. This means, they will allow you to release the past and look forward to the future you are creating!

We want you to understand that YOU can do this, no matter what's happened to you in your life. You, and only you, are solely responsible for your reactions and moving forward! So, let's create the best parenting heart EVER!

The heart activities will ask you to:

-Describe a parenting event related to the topic in the chapter, that you feel shaped who you are as a parent and why. Examples of significant events could be: births, birthdays, vacations, moves, sports, awards, graduations, deaths, divorce, remarriage, work changes, relationships, religious/spiritual ceremonies, first experiences, pets, gifts, immediate family members' events, school, concerts, conferences, injuries, workshops, etc. Pause to reflect on what events come to mind.

Rate the event on a scale of negative ten (–10) to positive ten (+10). Negative ten being the worst possible thing that could ever have happened to positive ten being the best possible thing to have ever happened. The zero is neutral. We will ask you to rate how you felt about the event at the time it was happening and how you feel about the event now. If it's a different rating, we will ask you what has changed.

Assess: whether you were responsible for the event and/or the outcome of the event.

Discuss: if you would change any of the events if you could.

Evaluate: any links between why you parent the way you do and the particular life event.

Decide: knowing what you now know, if you would want to change the course of your parenting life.

Amber Highlighted Stop Sign: Use Caution When Proceeding
There are three things you can do when you approach an amber light while you are driving: you can choose to slow down; observe the traffic around you and decide if you can make the light; or increase your speed, focused on your need to get wherever you are going. Which choice do you typically make?

Your parenting path is a journey; and maybe one of the most important journeys you take. We want you to be conscious of which choice you are making as you approach different parenting situations.

We'd like you to get to the place where you treat each amber highlighted stop sign with care. Meaning, that you will slow down, observe yourself and those around you. One of the biggest regrets parents share is that they wished for their kids to hurry through a certain phase of their life without appreciating what that phase offered them—time with their kids. We'd like to minimize your regrets and have you find appreciation in all the moments.

To help facilitate slowing down and appreciating each moment for what it is, each stop sign will offer some questions. Take some time to reflect on the questions and see where you can begin to make changes today, that will start correcting toxic behaviours in which you may be engaging.

Target: S.M.A.R.T. Goal Setting System

When you identify your most important goals, you begin to figure out ways you can make them come true. You develop the attitudes, abilities, skills, and financial capacity to reach them. You begin seeing previously overlooked opportunities to bring yourself closer to the achievement of your goals. This way of setting goals helps you understand that results are only going to come with action, and that there is a process.

Remember those stars you thought of earlier? Now think of the S.M.A.R.T. goal–setting approach like the bow that is going to launch your arrow to reach those stars!

Specific

Goals should be straightforward and emphasize what you want to happen. WHAT are you going to do? Use action words such as direct, organize, lead, coordinate, develop, plan, build, etc. WHY is this important to do at this time? What do you want to ultimately accomplish?

"I am going to read this parenting book and do the activities as I feel like parenting is the best and the worst thing that has ever happened to me."

Measurable

If you can't measure it, you can't manage it. Choose a goal with measurable progress, so you can see the change occur. How will you 'see' when you reach your goal? Establish concrete criteria for measuring progress toward the attainment of each goal you set. When you measure your progress, you stay on track, reach your target dates, and experience the exhilaration of achievement that refuels you. "I am going to complete a chapter a month, including reading the book and completing the steps in the workbook."

Attainable

A goal needs to stretch you slightly so you feel you can do it and it will need a real commitment from you. The feeling of success this brings helps you to remain motivated.

"I know that it's attainable for me to read and complete the questions for each chapter over a month time period. I will write this in my agenda at the beginning and end of each month."

Realistic

This is not a synonym for 'easy.' Realistic, in this case, means 'doable.' The goal needs to be realistic for you and where you are at the moment.

"This is a doable goal because with my current work schedule, family schedule, and my own personal schedule, I can make this happen in the given time frame. I will ensure my family knows that it's a priority for me."

Timely

Set a timeframe for the goal: next week, in three months, by fifth grade. Putting an end point on your goal gives you a clear target to work towards. If you don't set a time, the commitment is too vague. It tends not to happen because you feel you can start at any time. Without a time limit, there's no urgency to start taking action now.

"I will have completed this parenting book and its activities by December."

 Happy Face: Happy…Just Because
The line of success is not straight and not without its intense moments. Sometimes it's caused by our own actions and reactions and other times by things out of our control. Life is just like that. When you are thinking about reaching your parenting hopes, wishes and dreams, just remember, it won't be smooth sailing. Be ready for some choppy waters along the way.

Think of this like a movie that's just come out, that people have invested millions of dollars and years of time and energy into, and the reviews are awful. The designers, writers, actors, directors, etc. have a choice to have a 'pity party' or be happy…just because. You have this same choice in life. People aren't going to always like you, including your kids and yourself, but you have a choice to live in that moment or not.

When you shift to being happy 'just because,' you won't be waiting your whole life for something to happen, a whole list of things to be happy about, or for somebody else's approval. You will be living life on your terms!

Yes, you have permission to be happy without having to accomplish or obtain the next ten things on your To Do lists.

Now that you understand what makes up our *Success...With A Twist* System, are you ready to get TWISTED with us?

"Those who don't jump will never fly."

- Leena Ahmad Almashat

Ready, Set, GO!

This book journey is meant to make you start taking more responsibility for your choices and thoughts in relation to your parenting. Let's start to examine your current thought patterns and behaviours that are shaping the parent you are today.

Parenting Skills Questions

Amber Highlighted Stop Sign: Use Caution When Proceeding

Remember that the amber stop sign wants you to proceed with caution and observe yourself and others. I invite you to write down your answers to the following questions on a sheet of paper or in our *Parenting…With A Twist Workbook* (if you've purchased one.) If you are doing our Video Series, complete these questions before watching the corresponding video.

Star: Hopes, Wishes, Dreams & Desires

1. Think of yourself in a circle: this is the Circle of Comfort. This is where you are right now. Draw a circle and title it: The Parenting Circle of Comfort or refer to the page in your workbook.

2. Think of your dreams, goals, wishes, hopes and desires outside of the circle, as represented by stars.

a) Draw some stars outside your circle and label them dreams, wishes, hopes, and desires or refer to the page in your workbook.

b) Write down your parenting dreams, wishes, hopes, and desires beside these stars.

c) At the top of this paper, write: "I can reach these stars. I can be the parent I've always wanted to be."

d) Take a mental picture of this image or snap an actual photo and keep it on your computer or phone or make a print.

e) Share these dreams, wishes, hopes and desires with your Accountability Partner.

f) Visualize this mental image while you close your eyes. Don't open them until you truly feel that you can reach at least one of your stars.

Our journey together will be to help you reach those stars!

g) Anytime you start to feel discouraged as you read through the book or if you have a particularly challenging parenting moment, come back to this image. You can always reach out to us as well! (Our contact information can be found at the end of each chapter in the Parenting Skills Question section.)

Circles: Different Lenses We Put On

3. Where and from whom did you learn how to parent?

Heart: Life Experiences that Shape Us

4. a) List and describe any events you can remember that have shaped you to be the parent you are today.

b) Why did you choose these specific events?

c) Rate these events on a scale of negative ten (-10) to positive ten (+10). Negative ten being the worst possible thing that could ever have happened to positive ten being the best possible thing to have ever happened. Zero is neutral. Rate how you felt about the event at the time it was happening and how you feel about the event now. Is it a different rating?

d) Were you responsible for the event and/or the outcome of the event?

e) If you could, would you change any of the events?

f) Do you see any links between why you parent the way you do and these particular lifeline events?

Happy Face: Happy…Just Because

5. In order to shift from our past to our present and be able to clearly see our future, we need to release the past. I invite you to write a letter of gratitude to the people that you feel influenced you as a parent. I want you to write this from a place of understanding that they did the best they could with what they knew.

6. Decide what you are going to do with these letters. If it's a positive one, you may really want to share with the person. Where I want you to be conscious of in shifting to being happy…just because, is in the letters that might be negative. You want to acknowledge the negative influence simply to clear it from your past. You don't want to bring this negativity into your present parenting or into reaching for your parenting stars!

Target: S.M.A.R.T. Goal Setting System

7. a) Write a S.M.A.R.T. goal for completing this book.

b) Write a S.M.A.R.T. goal for one to three of your parenting stars from question #1.

Clapperboard: Miss Take versus Mistake & A.C.T. (Action Changes Things)

8. If you could change three things about your parenting, what would they be?

9. Share these answers with your Accountability Partner and, if you are comfortable, with your kids.

We are invested in your success, so please remember to connect with us

if you run into any difficulties or need any help with these questions.

**You can connect with us at our *Parenting… With A Twist*
Facebook page at Facebook.com/parentingwithatwist,
or click to parentingwithatwist.com**

"Time is your most precious gift because you only have a set amount of it. You can make more money, but you can't make more time. When you give someone your time, you are giving them a portion of your life that you'll never get back. It is not enough to just say relationships are important; we must prove it by investing time in them."

- Rick Warren

Parenting Tip #1
The Trouble is You Think You Have Time

Quality Versus Quantity

Quality time, not quantity of time when children are young, is a key factor in determining your child's success. The number of hours that parents spend with kids between ages three and eleven does little to predict the child's behaviour, wellbeing, or achievement. And actually, the more time you spend with them the more detrimental it can be on their long term success. Why? Because spending copious amounts of time with a child typically comes after feeling stressed about your already hectic day or out of feelings of guilt that you haven't spent enough time with them. This affects your child. It's referred to as "emotional contagion," the phenomenon where people 'catch' feelings from one another like they would catch a cold. So, if a parent is exhausted or frustrated, that emotional state could transfer to the children.

What does quality parenting time look like? It's engaging in one-to-one activities where you are lovingly and willingly giving your child your full attention. This would mean both you and your child putting down your electronic devices. Some examples of activities are: reading to your child, sharing meals, talking with them, and/or playing a game with them. Learn more about effective communication in order to make this time the best it can be in our chapter titled: "The Language of Leadership."

There is a strong correlation between positive outcomes for kids and the amount of parents' warmth and sensitivity toward their children.

Children also need time away from their parents. They need unstructured time to themselves without the engagement of parents, for social and cognitive development. Children form an understanding of the world around them through their experiences so time in other environments allows children to find discrepancies between what they already know and what they discover. This allows children to have success in the world as the world is not limited to the way one household runs; therefore, children adjust their ideas of the world and are adaptable.

Men Versus Women

Did you know that on average, mothers who work outside of the home today are spending as much time with their children as at-home mothers did in the early 1970s? As much time as stay-at-home moms…isn't it crazy what we do to ourselves as moms? This has led to mothers cutting back on sleep and time to themselves in order to lavish more time and attention on their kids. This adds to the strain of managing work, the commute, child care, activities and home demands, and the guilt of being away, making women snappish and always feeling rushed. Mothers often feel that they need to choose between themselves and their children, and there is guilt associated with choosing one's self.

Mothers' stress is related to poor outcomes for their children, including behavioural and emotional problems and even lower math scores.

In contrast, men don't experience the same level of guilt that working mothers feel and don't view caring for children as a source of stress. For men, having kids can boost their careers, while mothers pay a penalty.

Adolescents & Quality-Quantity Time

Interestingly, when a child becomes an adolescent, we typically think of them needing more time away from us (and us away from them.) The opposite is true. Quantity of time during adolescence, but still quality-based, is needed. The more time a teen spends engaged with their mother, the less delinquent behaviour. And the more time teens spend with both their parents together in family time, such as during meals, the less likely they are to abuse drugs and alcohol and engage in other risky or illegal behaviour. They also achieve higher math scores. The relationship with your child isn't built suddenly when they're teens, so be sure that you have formed a relationship with them early on.

Parenting Skills Questions

Amber Highlighted Stop Sign: Use Caution When Proceeding

How do you role model in the time you spend with your children? Role modelling is a way of signalling what's appropriate in terms of how you behave, what you do, the activities you engage in, and what you believe. Remember to share these answers with your Accountability Partner.

Clapperboard: Miss Take versus Mistake & A.C.T. (Action Changes Things)

1. Do you spend quality time with your child? If not, begin to find common fun activities to do together. Brainstorm with your child to find some activities and/or observe your child's actions.

a) Write these activities down in your notebook.

b) Schedule each activity into both of your agendas. (You all need to have agendas!)

2. a) Do you spend time with your child when you know your emotions have got the best of you? Just like you may not kiss them when you have a cold, please have the same awareness of their wellbeing when you are feeling stressed.

b) List some ways you can shift your mood or think of other solutions to 'contain the cold.'

Circles: Different Lenses We Put On

3. a) Do you consciously spend more engaged time with your teenager, or do you recoil at the thought of spending more time with your rebellious, attitude-driven teen? (If you're not at the teen years yet, think of another age or situation in which you've found it hard to want to spend time with your child.) Find common ground and engage at that level. Don't take the eye-rolling or the 'know-it-all attitude' personally. Remember, they are asserting who they are just as you did when you were a teen! Joke with them about this behaviour and share your stories of when you did that to your parents. And when all else fails, summon the image of them when they were at their sweetest and you felt only love for them. Be it at the moment they were born, when they wore the cutest outfit ever, or when you snapped a picture of them in just the right moment and caught them laughing. They are still that child!

b) Write down your favourite childhood moments of them and picture those when you go through your rough patches.

4. Even in knowing all of the above, you will still have times when you will feel you need to be the perfect parent and have an inner voice suggesting to you that you are doing it all wrong.

a) What would you tell your child who failed the first time they got up to ride their bike? Talk to yourself using that same gentle voice and giving the same message: "Try again! Everything gets easier with practice. You WILL ride that bike." And, we believe, you will become the parent of your dreams!

b) What is the toughest parenting moment you have experienced?

c) What is the best parenting moment you have experienced?

d) Choose which one you want to focus on. You have the power to decide which memory you want to hold on to. Choose wisely!

Heart: Life Experiences that Shape Us

5. a) Write a letter of forgiveness to yourself for a parenting mishap. Remember, you have the power to create your future. Don't let the past bring you down.

b) Are you open to sharing this letter with your child?

Target: S.M.A.R.T. Goal Setting System

6. a) Do you feel guilty if you spend time away from your children doing something just for you, then feel resentful towards your children because you don't take time for yourself? Start taking some self-care time. Embrace the feelings you have when you do spend time on yourself and be amazed at how it will contribute to spending quality, stress-free time with your children.

b) If you had unlimited time to spend on you, what would you do?

c) Choose one thing that you would do for yourself and set a S.M.A.R.T. goal for how you are going to achieve it.

We are invested in your success, so please remember to connect with us if you run into any difficulties or need any help with these questions.

You can connect with us at our *Parenting…With A Twist* Facebook page at Facebook.com/parentingwithatwist, or click to parentingwithatwist.com

"Money is only a tool. It will take you wherever you wish, but it will not replace you as the driver."

- Ayn Rand

Parenting Tip #2

My Mind On My Money, My Money On My Mind

Financially Ignorant Children

Keep in mind the statistics in relation to money—less than 31% of children between the ages of twelve and eighteen receive financial literacy information at school and only 1% of parents say their kids save anything from their allowance. Wow! We are sending our children off into the world completely ignorant about money. We are expecting them to be able to live on their own with no understanding of what savings, investing, spending, and budgeting even mean or look like in practice. No wonder they are leaving home only to come back until they are thirty-four!

Funny Money Mindsets

Another key factor to raising successful children is the thoughts that we ingrain in our children from a very young age about money. See if some of these resonate with you. Perhaps you heard them when you were a child and/or perhaps you say them to your children now.

"Money is the root of all evil."
-This implies that having money or wanting to attain money will make you bad.

"Money doesn't grow on trees."
-This implies that money is scarce.

"People only get rich by doing bad things or it's inherited."
-This implies that money is evil and is not obtained through working hard.

"Oh, they come from money."
-This implies that having money means they didn't have to work for anything.

"We've never been rich and will never be rich."
-This implies that you need money to make money.

"You can't get rich doing what you love."
-This implies that you just need to make money for the sake of making money but not for the pleasure the work brings you.

"It takes money to make money."
-This implies that if you don't have money, there isn't an opportunity to become wealthy.

"I don't understand money well enough to get rich."
-This implies that there is a limit on what someone can learn.

"Financial security comes from a having a good job and a steady pay cheque."
-This implies that you are limiting your career opportunities as they must fit into this definition of what financial security is.

"If you're rich in love, health and happiness, you don't need money."
-This implies that money is not a necessity.

And my favourite (from my childhood), "We can't afford that."
-This implies that money is scarce.

Each statement above is not right or wrong. However, they do each carry a judgement about money and shape our lens.

Why are these lenses not great for a prosperous, success-ready money mindset? If a parent is continuously telling a child, "We can't afford that." and/or "Money doesn't grow on trees," and are living as though money is scarce, then they are setting their child up to believe that there is only so much money out there to be had. This can lead to a child not wanting to share their money. This mindset might cause a child to think that in order to obtain money it must be taken from somebody else. This can also cause a child to think that money must be spent right away because who knows when it will come again. A scarcity mindset will lead to these unhealthy thoughts and habits in relation to money.

When a child doesn't want to share their money, they will grow up with a competitive attitude about money and believe there isn't enough in the world to go around. Where would charities be if we all thought this way?

People with this mindset may also think of ways to take it from those who have it because there is only a limited supply of it. We see this in countries that have a large rich population and a large poor population with a small middle class. Why? The poor class has nothing to lose if money can only be attained in this way.

Then there's the child who won't spend any money unless it is absolutely necessary and will go without because of the fear of not having money again. Even with money in the bank, they are fearful that this money is all there is. As we have to spend money to live, day to day existence is stressful for someone which such a fear.

On the flip side of this, is the child who thinks that money must be spent because money is scarce. They end up not understanding how to save. They may live in highs and lows with money, and living in highs and lows about anything does not make for a very happy and healthy existence.

Yes, as a parent, what you say about and how you treat money will form your child's relationship to money. And because actions speak louder than words, make sure your actions are congruent with what you say.

What if, instead, you said the following?:

"It is okay to want money. It is not greedy."

"It is okay to waste money and have luxuries as there is more than enough in the world for everyone."

"Money can make people happy."

"There are not certain people who get rich because they are 'lucky.' Everybody can attain that status."

"I will not have money envy or judge those with money."

Again, each statement above is not right or wrong. However, feel the difference compared to the earlier money statements.

Shifting Our Mindsets

In our work at Parenting…With A Twist with families using our Twisted Success System, we have the honour to shift entire families' mindsets about money! This particular family that has given me permission to share their story had a scarcity mindset around money. The mom, Tara, had grown up being told, "We can't afford that." Tara wanted to change this mindset as it was limiting her, and that her daughter, Bella, was adopting the same unhealthy mindset. We invited Tara to look at the statements above and tell us the one that made her the most uncomfortable. She chose the following statement: "It is okay to waste money and have luxuries as there is more than enough money in the world for everyone."

In coaching this family, here's what we did to work on their scarcity money mindset: Tara and Bella loved fashion! They had never bought a fashion magazine because Tara looked at that as a waste of money. They would sign out the magazines from the library. Great service! But, then, they couldn't cut the pictures out, which they liked to do when they went shopping or put an outfit together. We invited Tara to subscribe to a fashion magazine that Bella and her could choose together. Typically, this would be seen as a waste of money so we knew she had to do a repetitive action for an extended period of time in order to break this mindset. The science to back this up is called neuroplasticity. Neuroplasticity means that repetitive positive thought and positive activity can rewire our brains and strengthen brain areas that stimulate positive feelings. Our brains have the capacity to rewire themselves and/ or form new neural pathways when we do the work! Just like exercise, the work requires repetition and activity to reinforce new learning.

We told that them that every month when the magazine came in, they needed to be grateful that they could afford it and that because it was theirs, they could do what they wanted with it. The act of cutting pictures out helped them realize that it was okay to "waste" money. After three months of receiving the magazines, they saw financial abundance in other places in their life. By releasing their fears, their money mindset shifted as they now believe there is more than enough money to go around in the world.

What Allowance Teaches

Allowance gives you the opportunity to show your children how to manage money. Allowance in our house is divided into four categories: Savings, Spending, Investment and Giving Back. The money is divided by percentage into those categories. Spending is 40%, Savings is 40%, Investments is 10%, and Giving Back is 10%.

For spending, they are allowed to spend how they please under the $75 mark. They have to account for their entertainment needs/desires. They pay for their own meals out, as well as going to movies, etc.

Savings are for something that is over $75 and they need to have a plan as to how they will save enough money for it and do research on finding the best price for it. This also gives them time to decide if it's an impulse buy or it's something they truly need/desire.

Investment monies are to be put towards something that can help them gain more money than what they presently have. They could use it to pay for training or a license they need to secure work. For example, our son used his to take his refereeing course and our daughter, to take her babysitting course. It could be used towards printing fliers, advertising that your child is now a dog walker in the neighbourhood.

Giving Back monies are to be put towards a fundraising initiative, a cause they are passionate about, and/or a need they would like to help. We, as adults, are often asked to contribute towards fundraising, why not have your children involved in this decision-making process and in contributing? They can use it to donate towards their favourite causes.

If they don't have a favourite cause, it's an excellent project to research something they are passionate about it and see what they can do to help. Each family member could present to the rest of the family on their favourite cause to practise swaying other families to give to their cause. Family members can pool their money and use it to give back together.

If our child's Giving Back funds are depleted, they can always still participate with their time. For example, our family wanted to help more families at Christmas than we were financially able to, so we got involved with an organization that raises the funds but needs volunteers to do the shopping. We shopped for four families this past Christmas and we've voted that this way of giving back will become an annual tradition.

Family System: Non-Negotiables, Allowance, Chores & Family Rules

We suggest having an association between allowance and your family's non-negotiables, household chores, and family rules. Non-negotiables are a list of things that there is no compromising on, no arguing about. For example, in our house, brushing our teeth is a non-negotiable. Household chores are actions you have your child do around the house to help the house function. Taking the garbage out could be an example of a household chore. Family rules define how you want your family to treat each other. You could have a family rule that states that in your house nobody goes to bed mad. Please note that in the chapter titled: "Setting Up Your Household for Success," this system will be laid out in more detail. Our system works to tie these together without actually making one totally dependent on another.

Why did we design such a system? Our children wanted to start receiving an allowance and had heard that their friends were getting an allowance for doing chores. I didn't agree that an allowance was an expectation for doing something that helped the house run smoother. I don't get paid for taking out the garbage so why would my kids get paid for this? Also, aren't chores supposed to be making them a better person? That should be reward enough! People behave in certain ways to get them closer to what they need/desire. So, we tied allowance to the agreed upon non-negotiables, household chores and family rules. It is a win-win in that it brings children closer to getting money which is something they need/desire. Also, it allows a household to run more smoothly when parents are able to gently remind a child that there is a consequence that directly affects them, should they choose not to participate. As shown above, allowance is super important in teaching your children about money!

Income Levels Of Single Mothers

Income levels affect how success-ready a child is. Low-income mothers have more financial and day-to-day stress and feel they don't have the resources to keep up with intensive parenting expectations. We are focusing on single mothers in this section as we already learned in the chapter titled: "The Trouble Is You Think You Have Time" that it's a mother's stress that has more of an impact on a child than a father's.

Thankfully, we now know about quality time so this should help to alleviate some of the stress. However, statistics show, more than any quantity or quality time, income and a mother's educational level are most strongly associated with a child's future success. To support all children to be their very best, low-income mothers need to be encouraged to access their community's resources. These resources can aid both mother and children to support a healthy mental and physical state while compensating for the socio-economic status differences.

Gainful Employment

Adult children living at home cannot find gainful employment, nor have the financial ability to life on their own. The workforce looks for people with more than just degrees. Google discovered that the most successful employees are candidates who have demonstrated resilience and an ability to overcome hardship. They look for candidates who feel like they can take risks, can understand the team's goals, are engaged in what they are doing, are critical thinkers, have excellent communication skills, and possess the ability to trust others. Why? Because work groups do better when members are motivated to help each other. 'Who' is on a work team matters less than how the team members interact, structure their work, and view their contributions.

This can be quite confusing to the child who felt they were 'special' in school. So, to be successfully independent in adult life, we have to know how to have relationships with people, as well as how to be financially savvy. Where are these skills taught? We answer this crucial question in depth in the chapter titled: "What You Need To Be Success Ready."

Be Aware Of How You Spend Your Money

How much money you have versus how you spend it, is another way to look at how you are shaping your child. Does the way you spend it create connections, contribute to the world, have patience built in, meet the psychological needs of sharing, caring, and giving you a sense of who you are? When you spend your money are you a "janitor of your own possessions" (Frank Lloyd Wright), or do you use your money in ways that improve our world and, as a bonus, supply you with genuine and long-lasting connections?

Parenting Skills Questions

Amber Highlighted Stop Sign: Use Caution When Proceeding

How do you role model your money mindset and your actions around money? Role modelling is a way of signalling what's appropriate in terms of how you behave, what you do, the activities you engage in, and what you believe. Remember to share these answers with your Accountability Partner!

Circles: Different Lenses We Put On

1. a) Where does your understanding of money come from?

b) If you feel you don't have a solid understanding of how money works in relation to savings, investing, spending, and budgeting, how are you going to teach your child this? (Hint: invest in books or a money coach!)

2. How do you talk about money with your children? Be conscious of how you talk about money as it will shape your child's outlook.

3. a) When looking over these beliefs and associations that I've listed at the beginning of this chapter, which ones resonated with you? This is how you can determine what your current beliefs and associations around money are.

b) Are your beliefs empowering or disempowering? Do they help you or limit you?

Clapperboard: Miss Take versus Mistake & A.C.T. (Action Changes Things)

4. a) What are you actions around money? In other words, how do you role-model savings, spending, investing and giving back?

b) Are your words and actions in harmony? A child's outlook will be shaped by actions more than by words.

c) What is one action you can change starting today?

5. a) How do you spend your money? (Remember from this chapter: Does the way you spend it create connections, contribute to the world, have patience built in, meet the psychological needs of sharing, caring, and giving you a sense of who you are?)

b) Another way to think of this: when you spend your money are you a "janitor of your own possessions" or do you use your money in ways that improve our world and, as a bonus, supply you with genuine and long-lasting connections?

6. a) Are your children given an allowance?

b) How do they earn this allowance?

c) How is this allowance divided up when given to them? Do you have categories such as Spending, Saving, Giving Back and Investing that their money is divided into? In other words, what are you teaching them about money in giving them an allowance?

d) If they are not given an allowance, how are you teaching them to manage money?

Target: S.M.A.R.T. Goal Setting System

7. Define a S.M.A.R.T. goal for any of the above questions that you'd like to change.

Happy Face: Happy...Just Because

8. List three resources in your community that provide information in relation to money management or in relation to getting help if you are low income. (Start now as you will be teaching your child how to ask for help when they need it and how to seek out the appropriate resources.)

We are invited in your success, so please remember to connect with us

if you run into any difficulties or need any help with these questions.

You can connect with us at our *Parenting...With A Twist* Facebook page at Facebook.com/parentingwithatwist, or click to parentingwithatwist.com

"A person is both wise and wealthy
when they master the art of appreciating
what they already have."

- Zelig Pliskin

Parenting Tip #3
You Are Already Wealthy

Do you think of yourself as wealthy? Do you tell your children that you are wealthy? What if you looked at defining wealth differently?

Live To Work

I grew up in Toronto and had aspirations to be wealthy. This, to me, meant owning a beautifully decorated detached house, driving a nice car, having a Monday-to-Friday job with benefits, taking my allotted vacations every year in cottage country and dressing my kids in cute Gap outfits. If you flip back to the "funny money" statements from the beginning of the last chapter, can you identify which ones were said to me? If you suggested, "money doesn't grow on trees," "financial security comes from a having a good job and a steady pay cheque" and "we can't afford that," you are correct.

By age twenty-two, I had bought my own condo that I traded in two years later for a townhouse and then two years later traded that in for a semi-detached house. The semi-detached house was beautifully painted and filled with lovely furniture. I was on my way to a detached house. I drove a brand new, canary yellow Mazda 5. I worked as a high school teacher, which was perfect, as it was a secure, government, Monday-to-Friday job with benefits. I had vacations with my son in cottage country. And while my son was still letting me dress him, he wore cute, matching Gap outfits. I even have the pictures to prove it!

I worked hard. All through high school and my two degrees in university I worked one to three jobs. Once I was a teacher, I took extra courses to go up in the pay scale. I taught night school and summer school. I went back to work when my first son was only four months old. I was always researching and implementing leading-edge ways of teaching, curriculum, and brand new programs within our school system. I commuted two cities over which equalled a 90-minute commute each way to work each day to be able to afford the house I had. I was good with my money, in that I didn't indulge in a lot of extras and my only debt was my mortgage. So, I didn't "have to have" a Starbucks latte every day or the newest Coach purse. However, I did see the majority of people who surrounded me were certainly in the wheel of wealth attainment that seemed so elusive: they just got the one thing you had to have and the next thing popped up. And, everybody had debt. I was the exception. But I didn't really live life; I lived to work so I could support the life I thought I was supposed to have.

My children's father and I, for a variety of reasons, moved from Ontario to British Columbia in 2006. My children were 6 years old and 6 months old at the time. I was under the impression that I would get a teaching job; we'd use the money we sold the house and furniture for in Ontario to buy a new house and furniture, and we'd again go on to building the same life we had in Ontario.

When Life Happens

Then, life happened! My children's father and I separated. The bank account that held our house money was nearly empty. I was told I wouldn't get a teaching job in BC until people started retiring which wouldn't be for years. I ended up renting a two bedroom apartment with fifty-year-old furniture that was above an old mechanic's shop, where the mechanic used to live. It was beyond filthy. I started a training business from scratch, which meant no secure work, pay or benefits.

Through this process, my eldest son asked me if we were poor. In that split second I had before answering him, I realized that my attitude needed to change. So, while holding back the tears, I knew that I needed to find other ways to define wealth. I suggested to my son that I felt wealthy, in that:

- I had time with him and his brother, every single day! There was no rushing to work for a certain time or to commute every day. Instead, I had that time with them before and after school. I could attend their special functions at school. I could be there for them when they were sick or needed a mental health day.

- I got to do what I love every day, which is help people. I was creating a company based on my skill sets and the needs I saw in society. I was building a company in which people saw the value in what I was creating. This was a truly amazing experience!

- We lived in the most beautiful place; ocean and mountain views pretty much no matter where you were. Skiing and swimming in the same day. More parks than you can imagine. A country feel with city amenities. A place where everybody knows your name. A community where you can feel connected everywhere you go.

- We had access to resources that helped us so that the children could still participate in their extracurricular activities.

- I got to explore my potential every day in my work. Building a company from the ground up there is always something new to be learning and creating. While pleasure can disappoint, possibilities do not!

- I had the freedom to think for myself and decide what was best for us as a family, not have it dictated to me. So, if we needed a vacation, not in the prescribed time you get as an employee, we were able to take that time. (I'm writing this in Mexico in April where I took my ten-year-old son for his birthday!)

- We all had our health and access to community programs which ensured that we could get our basics, like teeth cleaning and counselling, covered.

- We had amazing friends and family. It was a friend who found our apartment, and another friend secured the furniture for us.

In my son asking me this question, I realized that how I defined wealth previously was based on the constant striving for material possessions. Even though I didn't think I defined my life like that, especially in comparison to those around me, I was modelling that for my children. My child thought he was poor because we had less material possessions and that was directly related to how I was acting.

Shifting Your Mindset

My sons and I started writing a nightly gratitude journal so we could shift our mindset by looking at all we did have.

Gratitude, the feeling of appreciation or thanks, has gained a lot of attention in the field of positive psychology. Studies have found that those who are habitually grateful are significantly happier than those who are not. Studies suggest that feelings of gratitude may even have health benefits. Positive psychology strives to develop methods by which one can consistently enhance gratitude levels. A very popular method is the maintenance of a gratitude journal.

A Gratitude Journal

A gratitude journal is a diary of things for which one is grateful for. Gratitude journals are used to help someone focus on the positive things in their lives! Studies have found that those who are habitually grateful are significantly happier than those who are not. Remember when we talked about brain neuroplasticity in an earlier chapter? To jog your memory, neuroplasticity means that repetitive positive thought and positive activity can rewire our brains and strengthen brain areas that stimulate positive feelings. So it's not surprising that having a gratitude journal is beneficial.

As we did our nightly gratitudes and wrote them down in our journal, all l the ways wealth showed up in our life became apparent: our family, our friends, where we lived, our health and abilities, the overflow of love we received, our new-to-us decorated home, the generosity of others, the love for what I did every day that I got to share with my family, the resources that enabled us to live an amazing life with very little financial resources; and lastly, for every breath we took as we lie down each night. There is no right or wrong way to do gratitude journals. You can do them in point form in your book. Some members of our house prefer to write them on their electronic devices.

Affirmation

When our children are having a tough time coming up with a gratitude, we get curious as to what thoughts they are having that are limiting them. When a person repeats negative thoughts, it steals their motivation and confidence. It is hard to feel motivated when you feel skeptical about getting any results.

Our daily beliefs and habits result from our repeated thoughts. If our child isn't able to come up with something they are grateful for because they are in such a negative space, we need to replace these negative thoughts with positive ones and use affirmations to do so.

An affirmation is a wish stated as if it is already true. Think of this like an advertising jingle that you are creating for your life. Thinking, saying, or writing affirmations are an easy way to bring about positive change. It is important to not use the negative thought words found below in your affirmation.

> *When a person repeats negative thoughts, it steals their motivation and confidence. Our daily beliefs and habits result from repeated thoughts.*

Positive Word Choices

Here's a list of word options for changing negative thoughts to positive thoughts:

Negative Thoughts If These Words Are Being Thought:	Positive Way to Change The Thought Use These Words Instead:
lack	abundance
fear	faith
depression	bliss

Negative Thoughts If These Words Are Being Thought:	Positive Way to Change The Thought Use These Words Instead:
hate	love
rage	calm
loneliness	harmony
emptiness	creativity/wonder
discouragement	enthusiasm
worthlessness	worthiness/perfection
shame	proud
dumb/weak	acceptance/learning/growing/wise
insecurity	confidence

Dig Deeper

Let's say your child says, "I'm dumb." Dig deeper to find out why. If it turns out that they are saying this because they didn't answer in class as quickly as somebody else, you could have them write: "I accept who I am and how I learn." This affirmation could be written in their agenda, in their gratitude journal, or even on a sticky on the bathroom mirror! You want it in a place where they can see it on a daily basis.

A child expresses fear about an upcoming test. As their affirmation, they could write: "I have faith that I will do my best." Remember, affirmations are like commercials to yourself about yourself. They also help redirect and eventually turn off, any negative self-talk!

My youngest son gave me one that says: "You are always beautiful." It's on green fluorescent paper and rests on the dashboard of my car. It's a great affirmation for me for anytime I am hard on myself in relation to my appearance. It makes me smile every time I get into the car!

Amazing results in life come when we change our habits. Our habits change when we have a change in attitude. Affirmations and gratitudes are a way we can change our attitudes. As you adopt more positive attitudes and feel encouraged, your actions and habits will shift.

Redefining Wealth

How about redefining wealth as the ability to fully experience life? By redefining the definition of wealth, I was able to show my son and myself that what we did have couldn't be taken from us, unlike material possessions. We also learned that one can flourish with very little material possessions, when they have everything I shared earlier. Plus, we developed a new habit that could carry him through tough times in the future: a gratitude journal. No matter what, you can always find things to be grateful for when you go to bed at night. As we know, life can throw us come curve balls and having a strategy to deal with those curve balls and come out smiling, amidst the tears, is crucial to mastering your happiness.

Past Versus Present

It's important to not get stuck in the past or caught up in the future; you miss the precious moments that make up our lives. Human nature is unappreciative of what is in the moment as we are conditioned to have attachments to things in the past and to focus on what we desire in the future. This keeps us in a revolving world of pain. When you are stuck in the past, you will not be able to enjoy the moment you're in or potentially even see a future. What if I didn't do 'x'? What if my parents hadn't done 'y'? You need to let go of 'x' and 'y'! I'll be happy when I buy these new shoes, that new TV, a new car, the dream house. The list can go on forever, if you are always waiting for life to happen or for the next phase of it to be attained.

Now I look at what I 'have' and I am filled with awe every single day. I wouldn't trade it for any of the financial security I had in my past. I'm truly thankful every day for the wealth that we do have. If you asked my son today, I'll bet he'd say we weren't poor anymore!

Finding Happiness In the Bills You Pay

I invite you to think about how you pay your bills and how you talk to your children about bills. Often people pay their bills like it's the last thing they want to do. And the stress that is associated with having to pay an unexpected bill is even greater. What if you were to pay your bills with gratitude? Gratitude that you have heat and hot water. Gratitude that you have a car to drive. Gratitude because you are supporting companies that employ people which enables those people to pay their bills. As bills are a reality, set your child up with a healthy mindset about them. Imagine how much stress you could alleviate from their life just by shifting this!

Parenting Skills Questions

Amber Highlighted Stop Sign: Use Caution When Proceeding

How do you role model your mindset in regards to wealth? Role modelling is a way of signalling what's appropriate in terms of how you behave, what you do, the activities you engage in, and what you believe. Remember to share these answers with your Accountability Partner!

Clapperboard: Miss Take versus Mistake & A.C.T. (Action Changes Things)

1. Overcoming adversity is a skill that companies look for when hiring someone. As you want your child to move out long before they are thirty-four years of age, what habits are you helping your child develop to teach them how to be resilient? (Hint: affirmations and gratitude journal are two examples.)

Happy Face: Happy…Just Because

2. a) Take the next expected bill you get and share three positive things about that bill with your child.

b) Challenge yourself to do this with the most unexpected bill you've received recently, as these bills usually cause us the most stress.

Circles: Different Lenses We Put On

3. a) How are you wealthy?

b) Share this with your child.

Heart: Life Experiences that Shape Us

4. a) Describe an event and/or person involving money from your past that is keeping your focus there.

b) Are you holding off on life waiting for the next purchase or financial life phase to make you happy?

c) Do you race through your life with work as a main focus to get a reward that will come to you when you retire at sixty-five, if all goes according to plan?

d) If you've answered "yes" to any of the three above questions, I invite you to stop racing and start living. What are five things you can focus on which only involve the present?

Target: S.M.A.R.T. Goal Setting System

5. Write a S.M.A.R.T. goal to incorporate the practice of gratitudes into your daily life.

We are invited in your success, so please remember to connect with us

if you run into any difficulties or need any help with these questions.

**You can connect with us at our *Parenting... With A Twist*
Facebook page at Facebook.com/parentingwithatwist,
or click to parentingwithatwist.com**

"If we expect kids to be losers they will be losers; if we expect them to be winners they will be winners. They rise, or fall, to the level of the expectations of those around them, especially their parents and their teachers."

- Jamie Escalante

Parenting Tip #4
Liking The Child You Love

Kid, You'll Move Mountains

The expectations parents hold for their kids have a huge effect on attainment. The Pygmalion Effect states, "What one person expects of another can come to serve as a self-fulfilling prophecy." This means that when you hold a certain belief about how somebody will turn out, you are shaping them to turn out in that way. So, let's all hold the expectation that our children will be success-ready!

Fixed Versus Growth Mindset

A "fixed mindset" assumes that our character, intelligence, and creative ability are traits that we are unable to change in any meaningful way. Success is, therefore, the affirmation of that inherent intelligence, our strive for success, and our avoidance of failure at all costs. If kids are told that they aced a test because of their innate intelligence that creates a fixed mindset.

A "growth mindset" thrives on challenge and sees failure not as evidence of non-intelligence, but as a springboard for growth and for stretching our existing abilities. At the core is a distinction in the way you assume your will affects your ability, and it has a powerful effect on kids. If they succeeded because of effort, that teaches a "growth" mindset. To raise a success-ready child, you will need to ensure that you are focused daily on seeing your child through the 'growth lens.'

Love Your Child, Re-Direct Their Behaviour

From an early age, children's behaviours are primarily to please their caregivers and to have their own needs met. If your child is acting in an undesirable way, address the need behind the behaviour with love. Then, redirect the behaviour. For instance, when a child is hungry, give them the language to ask for food and teach them to understand when their body may be giving them signs that they indeed need food. "When you are feeling like you are short tempered, think about the last time you ate something. If it's been awhile and you can tell your short temper is coming from hunger, then please use your words to tell me this."

In my case, I get 'hangry' (angry when I'm hungry) when I don't eat, so it's super important for me to know the signs and to either have food available or ask for some. Every child is different so start to help them monitor when they last ate to see if food could be the reason behind being short tempered or having a lack of focus. Instead of having your child get to the point where they are 'hangry' give them the following tools: If they get to the point where they are having a meltdown and it's simply because of being hungry, address the need for food. When they are on an even level again, redirect their behaviour for next time, as suggested above. Depending on the age of your child, you would teach them to use verbal or non-verbal cues to tell you. Your child's age, as well as their personality, would determine how you would approach the redirection. With a younger child, you may pack snacks for them if you know you are going to be doing errands and may not be back in time for their next meal; whereas, with an older child, you may remind them that they may want to pack a snack. With a child that likes a lot of choice, you may want to leave the snack that they choose, open-ended; whereas, with a child that doesn't like a lot of choice, you may want to give them two options of which snack to choose from!

Your kids are driving you crazy; what do you do? Redirect the behaviour while still showing love for who they are as a person. Children's misbehavior is often unintentional or has a reason behind it. Children get a lot of feedback on their behavior by how we (adults) react. If something gets minimal attention it's likely a child won't do it again unless they got something out of it. On the other hand, if they get your attention then they may do that very thing to get your attention again!

Remember our analogy of a child learning to walk: we clap for them and make a big deal out of it so they continue to try. All that encouragement tells them they are doing something right. It also has the same effect when we react to misbehaviour. So, redirection simply gives us, as parents, another option to saying "no."

We can choose to use a calm voice to redirect them to a more appropriate activity or offer them choices. For instance, when my son wanted to run through the mall, I would suggest that he could march or walk. I modelled marching and walking, as children will learn more through our actions than our words. So, if you are yelling at your child to stop yelling at you, chances are they will continue to yell at you. In this case, you could redirect their behaviour by whispering your response to them!

Using redirection as a communication strategy, as opposed to reacting, was introduced to me in my first year of university when I was completing my Social Work degree. While the science students at my university had science labs with beaker cups and other science related objects, the other social work students and I had a three hour communication lab every Monday morning. Our communications lab didn't have any beaker cups or the like, we had chairs that we all sat in and faced each other – one big, happy circle! It was quite the way to wake up on a Monday morning at school. I won't forget the moment where I realized that as a social worker, I'd have to work with someone whom I disagreed with and sometimes might even be offended by their behaviour. And not only work with them, but truly support them on their journey. How was I going to do this? It was my first real taste of correcting one's behaviour and still showing love to the person.

People Treat Us How We Let Them

People also treat us how we teach them to. Be aware that along the way, you've taught your child to treat you in a certain way to get what they need (this can extend to all your relationships.) If your child realizes that the best way to get your attention is to have a meltdown, you've just taught your child that the best way to get your attention is to have a meltdown. Remember: what you feed, grows. Whether it's positive or negative attention doesn't really matter to the child who just needs a moment of your time. Give them the attention then

Love your child, and redirect their behaviour.

redirect their behaviour, and soon the meltdowns will stop. You will be teaching your child how you want to be treated while meeting their needs.

What You Feed, Grows

A really simple way to think about which kind of mindset you have, a fixed or a growth mindset, is by remembering: what you feed, grows. Decide what you want to grow in your child!

When you think about it, children's needs, right from conception, are fairly simple: love, nutrition and cleanliness! Don't see their behaviour as the predestined way they will be for life, or withhold their need because you don't enjoy the way they are expressing it. It's very damaging for a child to hear that their behaviour defines who they are. If you are going to start defining your child from an early age, share the positive stories about them.

Children are not robots that turn on when you press a button or reboot because you press a series of buttons. We must stop holding children to a higher standard of perfection than we can attain ourselves. Unless you do hold yourself to unrealistic perfection standards, and that's a whole other book you need to read!

Miss Take Versus Mistake

Anxiety is on the rise. Why? Children are afraid to make a mistake. I invite you to start spelling the word "mistake" like this: "miss take." When a child is learning to walk, they have several takes before they get it right. In other words, they have several "miss takes" before they can walk. We encourage them to make a miss take and get back up again. We help them get up when they fall. We set them up for success by blocking stairs where they could get hurt.

Later, they move on to school, where miss takes are graded and reported on. Instead of looking at a low mark and seeing how to help the child rise from that, it's used to shame children, compare children and make children afraid. "Get good grades or else!" "Why can't you be more like your sister?" We need to not let miss takes define us, but to grow us!

Great Relationships Are Not Born

When my clients ask me, "How can I ensure that I raise the best child?" I reply, "Don't worry about raising the best child—concentrate on becoming the best parent you can be!"

Great relationships are not born, they are created. Let's stop and think of love like a magnificent bonfire. They are not born, they are created. To start, they need the right mix of components to ignite and then a process to keep burning. If you ask people what those components are and what the process is to keep a fire burning, there could be quite a few different answers. The key here is that there's no right or wrong answers, just different answers. You and your child are two separate human beings, so be aware of this when you are spending time with them. You may have to remember back to when you were a kid and engage in a game of Tag. On the flip side, they may join you for something you like to do. As you go through this book, you will find new and creative ways to engage with your child.

In acknowledging and understanding that there are differences between yourself and your child, there are still very specific things that fire does need to ignite and keep burning. Love is like that. There are certain components that need to be present and a process that needs to occur. A bonfire might go out if you remove certain components, just like in a relationship. If key components are removed, the love might go out.

What is this magical key component that both fires and relationships have in common? They both need to be constantly fed! And, while we know kids need to be fed copious amounts of food, especially growing ones, in this case we mean a commitment to the relationship. Are you constantly feeding your relationship with your child?

Commitment to Continuously Rebuild

Keep in mind that sometimes the fire does go out or is reduced in size, but it's the commitment to continuously rebuild it that sustains it or gets it going again. This might be because a key factor is missing or is out of everybody's control, like rain came along and put it out. This is the same in a relationship, so it's important to gauge your commitment level to rebuild if a component of your relationship changes. What if your child got a failing grade? What if your child broke a house rule? What if you decide to get remarried? What if the two of you had an argument and both said hurtful things? You have to be committed to continuously building the relationship—no matter what!

As a bonfire needs to have oxygen, love needs to have some breathing room as well. To ensure the time you spend together is quality time, both parties need to spend some time apart as well. You don't want to smother each other.

Two people involved in a committed relationship have to choose that commitment level again and again as they evolve. So, as your cute-as-a-button baby turns into the Terrible Two's or the Crazy Tweens, you still have to love them. But there is nothing to fear from this kind of choice and change. Renewing one's commitment to one another through times of change will revitalize it.

Relationship Bank Account

Did you know that for every criticism, it takes six times the amount of praise to erase that one critical comment? Think of your relationship with your child like your bank account. You have debits and credits. Debits are the negative comments and credits are the positive comments that show you are grateful for what they do, rather than what they don't do. Watch how many debits you are depositing in your relationship bank account versus how many credits.

Children can't see and live up to the best in themselves if we're always pointing out the worst in them. Correct without criticism. Because, remember: what you feed grows! Contact us for examples of helpful comments you can use to correct without criticism. (Our contact information can be found at the end of each chapter in the "Parenting Skills Question" section.)

In order to maintain a healthy relationship bank account, there are two pitfalls to be aware of:

One is, you don't want to have a mental list of everything they have done wrong as you work on correcting a behaviour. And if you do, you certainly don't want to share your list with them. Correct their behaviour with love. For instance, if they forgot to put their dinner dishes away, you don't want to list all the things they've forgotten to do in the last week, year or month! Tempting as that may be, it doesn't feed or grow your relationship bank account in a very positive way. (By the way, this works with your spouse as well!)

The other, is living in the past instead of correcting a pattern of behaviour. For example, you've worked with your child on putting their dirty laundry in their hamper and they have accomplished it. When they don't do it six months later, don't bring up the past.

There is no such thing as perfect parents, children and families. But take comfort in the fact that you are perfect at being you. And your child is perfect at being them.

Parenting Skills Questions

Amber Highlighted Stop Sign: Use Caution When Proceeding

How do you role model during the time you spend with your children? Role modelling is a way of signalling what's appropriate in terms of how you behave, what you do, the activities you engage in, and what you believe. Remember to share these answers with your Accountability Partner.

Circles: Different Lenses We Put On

1. a) What self-fulfilling prophecy are you setting your child up for?

b) Describe your child as you describe them to others.

c) How do you describe them to themselves?

2. a) Do you have a growth mindset or a fixed mindset for your child?

b) Do you have a growth mindset or a fixed mindset for yourself?

3. Are you expecting your child to be a robot who can be 'fixed' by a simple reboot? Be honest!

Clapperboard: Miss Take versus Mistake & A.C.T. (Action Changes Things)

4. a) Have you taught your child to treat you with respect?

b) Do you model what respect looks like when you and your child interact as well as when they interact with others?

5. a) Do you meet your child's needs in a loving way?

b) Do you redirect their undesirable behaviours?

c) Are you able to separate your child from their behaviour?

6. Are you allowing your children to fail? Picking them up when they fall and setting them up for success as they move forward?

Heart: Life Experiences that Shape Us

7. Do you have a positive or a negative balance in your relationship bank account with your child?

Target: S.M.A.R.T. Goal Setting System

8. a) Write a scenario in which you were having an issue with your child.

b) What is your child's need?

c) What is your need?

d) What is the natural consequence of both needs not being met?

e) What can you do differently and/or the same?

We are invested in your success, so please remember to connect with us if you run into any difficulties or need any help with these questions.

You can connect with us at our *Parenting… With A Twist* Facebook page at Facebook.com/parentingwithatwist, or click to parentingwithatwist.com

"Coming together is a beginning;
keeping together is progress;
working together is success."

- Henry Ford

Parenting Tip #5
Setting Up Your Household For Success

Expectations

We've talked about unreasonable expectations of our children, but before you think that I don't believe in having expectations at all, let's address this. You want to have expectations and you want to have them evolve out of the growth mindset explained in the last chapter. You want them to strive to set goals and accomplish them.

Expectations build a child's self-esteem by holding them accountable and by sending them the message that you know that they are capable of doing better. Such expectations tell children that they possess the ability to behave, tolerate disappointment and frustration, delay gratification, grow, and do better—all of which builds their self-esteem.

Entitlement Versus Privilege

Sometimes parents get so caught up in giving to their children that they overlook what power they do have. It is important to understand the difference between a parental obligation and a child's privilege. We are obligated to provide food, schooling, medical care, shelter, and respect. In different people's homes, privileges may look different, but a partial list is: special foods, private schooling, extracurricular activities, vacations, television, and electronics.

By getting clear about what is a privilege, you can do a better job with discipline and curbing a sense of entitlement in your children. For example, in your home, and therefore, in your opinion, a child may need a cell phone for specific reasons. This cell phone would have certain restrictions on it in terms of usage that fit with what you feel is needed. It would then be a privilege to have anything over that. You could explain to your child that if they feel titled to more minutes than what is on the plan, then they pay for the extra amount.

In our house, our children don't have cell phones because we feel that's a privilege that if they want, they can pay for. Their electronics are also a privilege, which we can use our power as the adults in their lives, to make restrictions around. If we made restrictions around how many times a week they were allowed breakfast that would be taking away from an obligation we have to feed them. But if they expected that we were going to get them an expensive protein powder, there could be a negotiation as to who's going to pay for that, as that's not necessarily a parental obligation.

What you don't want to do is give your children a life of overprotection, overindulgence, over-everything. The statistics about many of today's twenty- and thirty-somethings show that they are finding the real world just a little too real and are going back home to Mommy & Daddy where they aren't paying rent, buying groceries, or even cleaning and cooking for themselves. But, now that we know what we know, whose fault is that?

Household Chores

Household chores are an ideal place to teach a child about expectations: learning that work has to be done and that each one of us must contribute for the betterment of the whole. Kids raised on chores go on to become employees who collaborate well with their coworkers, are more empathetic because they know firsthand what struggling looks like, and are able to take on tasks independently. They think—"I have to do the work of life in order to be part of life!" As Google suggested, they are looking for employees with more than just degrees, but with these skill sets as well.

As parents, we have to let go of the lens that the chores will be done to our adult level of perfection. We need to allow children to make miss takes. Teach them how to clean a washroom or do laundry. Accept some miss takes, and think of what an amazing roommate or partner they will make later in life, leaving your house with these skill sets. Please reach out to us if you would like a copy of age-appropriate chores. (Our contact information can be found at the end of each chapter in the "Parenting Skills Question" section.)

Non-Negotiables

We all behave certain ways because we get something out of it. While we can be creative and understanding about someone's learning style and needs, we can still have a list of non-negotiables. This is a list of things that there is no compromising on, no arguing about, with a predetermined, natural consequence decided on and attached to it. Remember when creating this list, that you aren't raising a robot or a mini-you, so choose your battles and involve your child! What could be on this list? Please reach out to us if you would like a list of suggested non-negotiables.

To illustrate our point, let's use the example of brushing one's teeth before bed as a non-negotiable. For a younger child whom you have control over their eating, if this is not followed through on, there will be no sugary foods eaten. Not sure if you've checked the labels of foods these days, but almost everything has sugar in it! If not brushing continues or results in a cavity, especially for the older child that you don't necessarily have the same control over what they eat, then the child is responsible for paying for their own dental cleaning and/or cavity filling. You can remind your child of the already agreed upon consequence so that you don't argue about it—it just is.

Consequences

Let's talk about why we are suggesting a "natural consequence" versus a "just is" consequence. A natural consequence is something that would happen on its own if the desired behaviour wasn't followed. For example, the situation we gave above: if a child doesn't brush their teeth, chances are greater they will get a cavity. If a child forgets their coat at home on a rainy day, chances are greater that they will get wet. Natural consequences make sense, so when your child questions why they are getting a consequence, it's an easy explanation.

Make sure that you choose a consequence that you can and will enforce. Do your best to lay out consequences before having to enforce them. Have a family meeting about your non-negotiables and their consequences.

Consequences should be age appropriate. If you cannot come up with a natural consequence use a consequence that affects what they value the most. This could also be known as your child's 'currency.' Screen time is quite popular in our house as our children's currency.

One night at a restaurant during a holiday, I heard a dad say to his children, "You two will never have ice cream again if you don't sit down in your seat right now!" It was a fancy restaurant and now 7pm. We had seen the two and four year olds at the pool all day. Guess what we saw the next day? The two children eating ice cream. Before you ask, no, they didn't sit back down in their chairs the night before.

I'd like to make a few points about the above scenario that relate to the guidelines given for consequences:

• Never say never. (Yes, I realize I just said it twice!) Saying, "You are 'never' going to have ice cream again." to a two and a four year old sets you up for a lifetime of failure with enforcing that consequence. And, let's admit it, there are times when parents say that about a lot of things. "You will 'never' get this iPad back." "You will 'never' be allowed to see Johnny again." And truth be told, they get their iPad back and Johnny is over playing on it with them.

- It's not a natural consequence. What does sitting down and ice cream have to do with each other? Perhaps, if there was ice cream for dessert, and he said, "If you don't sit down, you aren't going to be able to have your dessert." that would have been more of a natural consequence.

- It's not age appropriate. Children of those ages couldn't care less about the future. All they care about is the now. They truly are going to have no recollection that they didn't sit down two weeks ago, or let's be realistic, even two minutes ago. So they will not relate not sitting to not getting ice cream.

- Bringing your two and four year olds to a fancy restaurant at 7pm when you've all had a full day in the sun is setting yourself and your children up for failure. Maybe if they had naps or maybe if the kids had gone to the kids' club and just the parents went out for that dinner—there are always solutions for having your ice cream and eating it too!

- If the children had been older and they were just bored, and you couldn't think of a natural consequence for that scenario, you could suggest that their screen time be increased for the next day or that night, if they could sit back down and engage as a family. Remember, consequences can also be positive! You've just used their currency, that is, if the children in your home like their screen time as much as the children in my home!

To further a harmonious household, alongside non-negotiables, we suggest defining household chores and family rules. Please reach out to us if you would like a list of examples of what your family could agree on in terms family rules.

Family Mission Statement

Family Rules are included here as they set the stage for your family. Think of them as your family's mission statement to the world! Interestingly, there is a significant correlation between children's social skills as kindergarten students and their success as adults two decades later. Socially-able children who cooperate with their peers without prompting, are helpful to others, understand their feelings and resolve problems on their own, are far more likely to earn a college degree and have a full-time job by age twenty-five over those with limited social skills. Figuring out how to ensure that our children know how to get along with others before even entering school is super important to the rest of their lives.

Parenting Skills Questions

Amber Highlighted Stop Sign: Use Caution When Proceeding

How do you role model this? Role modelling is a way of signalling what's appropriate in terms of how you behave, what you do, the activities you engage in and what you believe. Remember to share these answers with your Accountability Partner!

Clapperboard: Miss Take versus Mistake & A.C.T. (Action Changes Things)

1. a) Do you have expectations of your child?

b) Are your expectations reasonable?

c) Are they based on the uniqueness of your child?

2. a) Is there an expectation that your children develop good social habits?

b) How do you facilitate this?

3. a) What are the behaviours in your house that occur often that you would like to correct?

b) What is a natural consequence for each of these behaviours?

Target: S.M.A.R.T. Goal Setting System

4. Does your family have an agreed upon mission statement that dictates how people will treat each other?

5. Do you have an agreed upon list of chores and non-negotiables?

6. Write a S.M.A.R.T. goal to create a system like the one explained in this chapter that combines your family rules, household chores, non-negotiables and allowance.

We are invested in your success, so please remember to connect with us

if you run into any difficulties or need any help with these questions.

**You can connect with us at our *Parenting... With A Twist*
Facebook page at Facebook.com/parentingwithatwist,
or click to parentingwithatwist.com**

"If a child can't learn the way we teach, maybe we should teach the way they learn."

- Ignacio Estrada

Parenting Tip #6
Please Do Label My Child

Learning Styles: The Right Label

Do children even understand that how we learn could be a subject in and of itself? The way one child's brain learns is different than another child's brain. There isn't a course at school called, "How We Learn," yet every day, all day at school, children are supposed to be learning. Seemingly, learning means that as long as a child can memorize and regurgitate what they've heard, that they are deemed successful in school. As we've all seen, that doesn't equate to success in life.

Imagine if every child was taught as though they had a 'special need.' Other terms for special needs that you may be familiar with are: identification, label and designation. When a student has a special need, like ADHD (Attention Deficit Hyperactivity Disorder) that student has the right to have an Individualized Education Plan (IEP) written for them. In theory, the IEP is presented at a school-based team meeting. This team meeting has all the key people in the school system, along with the parents, that would need to be aware of and accountable for the outlined education plan. This IEP follows them through school, and the theory is that teachers read it and accommodate their teaching to how that child learns best. For example, in the IEP, an accommodation could be that the teacher gives the IEP'd student a copy of the teaching notes. This way the student with ADHD doesn't have to focus on simultaneously writing down what the teacher is lecturing on and learning it. They can just focus on simply hearing the teacher. Another accommodation might be noise-cancelling earphones or listening to music during desk work time. This way the student can be focused on what they are working on as opposed to the noises around them.

Next, imagine if the teacher was able to look at their class and think: each child I am teaching has a special need. And then taught them in a way that activates their brain. We call this: teaching to one mind at a time. How can a teacher do this with twenty-five kids in their class? Simple, they could have each child take a Learning Style Questionnaire. By labelling them by how they learn, classroom dynamics such as seating placement, teaching methods and assignment options could be tailored to the needs of the learners in the class. (I'm excited as this is the topic of the next book in our *Success...With A Twist Series–Educating... With A Twist*.)

Learning Style questionnaires can be found for free online; therefore, they are accessible to everyone. Please contact us and we will send you the questionnaires we recommend. (Our contact information can be found at the end of each chapter in the "Parenting Skills Question" section.) By comparison, if you want your child to receive a special needs label like those given by a specialized psychologist, it costs thousands of dollars, there is a wait list to get this kind of testing done, and there can be a certain stigma attached to having this label. Please note that we don't believe that there should be a stigma attached to any label; the title of this chapter is, "Please Label My Child"! However, we have dealt with numerous families that have shied away from having their child formally tested due to the perceived stigma they feel would follow their child through the education system with such a label.

Our point is that not all children learn the same; yet, in most school traditional public school systems, all children in the same grade are given the same textbook and the same workbooks. This would be one of the factors of the school system that assumes that all children learn the same.

In 2008, my son was mandated to read the novel, *The Outsiders*, for Grade 8 English. Guess what? In 1987, I was mandated to read the same novel in Grade 8 English. This would assume that the children of 2008 are the same as the children of 1987. In a span of twenty-one years, I believe we could all agree that society has changed (think back to the phones from twenty-one years ago); why hasn't the curriculum?

The Learning Style Questionnaires that we recommend and use with our families will test for the four dominant learning styles: visual, auditory, read/write, and kinesthetic. Can you guess which learning style most traditional public school systems use? If you guessed read/write you are correct! If you think about it, most teachers have always taught from a textbook (read) and expect answers to be written out (write) in their notebook or on a worksheet. This may have you wondering—what happens to all the other learners?

Teaching Style Versus Learning Style

What happens when a learner has a different learning style than the teacher is teaching in? The majority of learners we've worked with and schools we've worked in suggest that teachers proceed to answer the quest for help in the same way they had taught the lesson, which may mean all learners' styles are not being taken into account. I invite you to think of a time where you asked for help at school or when your child shared that they asked for help. How was this need addressed? I'm going to venture an educated guess that it was answered in the teacher's learning style or in the style in which the curriculum was laid out.

Let's think about this for a second. The teacher just taught how to do a math equation, referred to the examples in the textbook, and then asked the class to complete the assigned textbook questions. This is a classic teaching style. Johnny asks for help. The teacher goes back to the board example or the textbook example. The problem is that Johnny is a visual learner, so to truly understand it in a way that lights up his brain, he will need the equation represented visually, which can be through pictures or colours. It would be helpful if Johnny was allowed to use different coloured pen/pencils to write out his work, if he was able to doodle in a side column, and if concepts were explained with words that he could focus on drawing so that he 'sees' the concept.

Sally asks for help. The teacher goes back to the board example or the textbook example. The problem is that Sally is a kinesthetic learner, so to truly understand it in a way that lights up her brain, she will need the equation to be represented in a hands-on way. This could be through blocks or anything physical that she can touch/feel to understand. Also, Sally would benefit from sitting on a yoga ball when having to sit in class, from chewing gum, and from having the freedom to move when she needs to. Why? Her body needs movement to be able to focus. Sitting for long periods of time to absorb mass information is not doable for Sally. Hmm…how are these children typically labelled by the school system? Does the term ADHD seem familiar? What if it's not a 'condition' but that we aren't meant to sit for an entire day? And what if there are actual learners whose brain doesn't process information unless they are moving?

Jesse asks for help. The teacher goes back to the board example or the textbook example. The problem is that Jesse is an auditory learner, so to truly understand it in a way that lights up his brain, he will need the equation to be represented through dialogue. This could be done through a story, a debate, or Jesse explaining the concept back to the teacher. Jesse would benefit from sitting in a group where he could have an opportunity to be the teacher and/or hear another student's perspective on what they are learning and have an opportunity to share his.

There is actually a defined way of lighting up each of these learner's pathways. I invite you to reach out to us if you would like the link so that you can assess your child's learning style. This will enable you to figure out what kind of learner your child is. This could start a wonderful conversation about how, moving forward, your child can learn based on the strategies that you read about for their learning style! Share this information with other key people in their life. For instance, it would be helpful for a child's grandparent to know that their grandchild is a kinesthetic learner who needs to continuously move when you are talking to them. There is nothing rude about the child doing that when talking to them or even when sitting at the dining room table for dinner.

Take the test for yourself. It's good to be conscious of how you learn to see if you are expecting your child to learn in that exact way. If you are a read/write learner and school was easy for you perhaps you expect it to be that way for your child.

Advocate For Your Child

Once you define and understand your child's learning style, be an advocate for them to be taught in that learning style. Give them the language and the tools. And then teach them to advocate for themselves. Imagine your daughter, who is a kinesthetic learner, explaining to the teacher, "When I ask for help, I need you to show me with these blocks I have." You would be giving your daughter the gift of understanding how she learns and the language and tools she needs to be successful!

A really simple example that we often suggest to high school students is taken from an IEP of an identified ADHD learner. If you remember, one of the accommodations was that the teacher could make them a copy of the lecture notes. Why not do this with any student who finds lectures overwhelming?

Advocate for your child to receive the notes as this gives your child:

- The possibility to highlight key pieces the teacher emphasizes as opposed to being aware of everything the teacher is saying.

- The ability to have the teacher's notes in front of them and also personalize them for their learning style: a visual learner could personalize their notes by drawing pictures on the copy of the teacher's notes of the key concepts the teacher is focusing on.

- The opportunity just to listen to the teacher and absorb what is being said as opposed to having to write out notes and listen for understanding.

Think of your child's learning style and what could benefit them in the classroom based on what you now know.

Parenting Skills Questions

Amber Highlighted Stop Sign: Use Caution When Proceeding

How do you role model this? Role modelling is a way of signalling what's appropriate in terms of how you behave, what you do, the activities you engage in, and what you believe. Remember to share these answers with your Accountability Partner!

Clapperboard: Miss Take versus Mistake & A.C.T. (Action Changes Things)

1. a) What is your child's learning style?

b) What is your learning style?

2. With the knowledge from question #1,

a) what tools and strategies can your child use to make them more successful in homework and studying?

b) what accommodations can you ask your child's classroom teacher to set up to increase success in your child's learning style? Or, what language can you give your child to ask their teacher for these accommodations?

We are invested in your success, so please remember to connect with us

if you run into any difficulties or need any help with these questions.

You can connect with us at our *Parenting... With A Twist* Facebook page at Facebook.com/parentingwithatwist, or click to parentingwithatwist.com

"When Students cheat on exams it's because our School System values grades more than Students value learning."

- Neil deGrasse Tyson

Parenting Tip #7

How To Read And Discuss A Report Card, No Matter What The Grade

When we put this book through test reads, we were asked why we had parenting tips that were focused on school. We spend more time going to school and working than doing anything else and research shows that the majority of people are not satisfied in either area of their lives. Not only not satisfied but both school and work are having the complete opposite effect–they are causing people to disengage with life. We feel that both can be motivating and energizing and want to help make that your reality.

Raise your hand if you had moments at school where you received a mark that you thought wasn't great and you were applauded for it. When we've asked this of our audience in our speaking engagements, very few, if any, hands are raised.

Demystify Grades

An "A" is great for certain kids, but for some kids a "C+" is amazing. How do we not judge our kids for the grades they get? Better yet, how do we help our kids to not judge themselves compared to others?

Let me demystify grades for you! Our children's worth in school is evaluated against preset standards of excellence in both behaviour and performance. So, a grade is simply just a marker of where a student is in the item being evaluated in that given time frame. This could be illustrated in seeing a child's mark go from an "A" in Math on one report card, to a "C" on the next report card, in the same year! Their level of understanding of how Math is being evaluated, at that point in time, has lessened.

Why would a child's grade from report card to report card go from an "A" to a "C"? This might be because something in their personal life has changed; their current teacher does not teach to their learning style; they have to take on more responsibility and haven't been taught how to do that; they have a fear of asking questions; they have learned the art of procrastination; they have developed a dislike for the subject. Imagine (insert sarcastic tone)—that's ALL that could be going on! Yet, neither a test nor a mark, tell us any of those things. They only tell us what the child's understanding is of a theory or fact at the exact moment the test is given.

They have to manage their life outside of school—be it a single-parent home, a split-custody situation, a blended family, or a two-parent family and all the dynamics that go along with each house. For example, some children might question whether there will be a snack that they love in their cupboard while others question if there will be any food in their cupboard! Then, there are their extracurricular activities to manage. Start to look at your child's world as a whole, not as isolated pieces.

Also, remember how marks are typically assigned: they are based on the results of a set of evaluation criteria. And, every child in the class gets the same evaluation. If you lined up a group of different animals to test them on how well they climbed a tree, a dolphin would fail. Dolphins are thought of as one of the smartest animals and yet, they'd fail if they were given a preset evaluation with criteria that is outside their skill set. A dolphin would think of itself as stupid and a failure; how do you think our kids feel? Our way of evaluating all children in the same way is setting up some of the brightest children to fail.

Not understanding a certain math concept doesn't make anybody stupid; it simply means they don't understand that math concept. That's a difference worth remembering.

Remembering The Scary Statistics

Let's take a moment to review the statistics from the beginning of the book, regarding students between Grades 5 and 12:

- Only 1 in 3 students feel they are success-ready.

- Almost 50% of students lack hope for the future, reporting they feel stuck in their lives or discouraged about the future.

- Almost 50% of students are disengaged with school, reporting they feel non-engaged or are actively disengaged.

- Almost 70% of students do not receive financial literacy information at school.

Right now, instead of asking the question, "What Do I Want to be When I Grow Up?" your child is asking, "What Do I Want to be When I Give Up?" The sad conclusion is that schools are home to many psychological dropouts. Kids that are disengaged with school and with their futures. The disengaged and hopeless effect on the psyche influences elementary and high school performance, post-secondary preparedness, employment opportunities, and choices concerning engagement in high-risk behaviours. Why are these statistics a reality? Why is there a sense of hopelessness and disengagement? Because schools are based on an assessment which mostly measures test scores.

What Tests Don't Measure

Tests typically measure content taught in a specific subject. They don't measure persistence, curiosity, enthusiasm, courage, leadership, creativity, resourcefulness, self-discipline, sense of wonder, big-picture thinking, compassion, reliability, motivation, humour, empathy, sense of beauty, humility or resilience. Tests simply measure what students know about a specific subject at a point in time, in the midst of all the other factors present in their life. What if a doctor prescribed the same medication to everyone that came to see her? Wouldn't that be considered tragic? Tests were originally designed in 1914 to weed out people that were eligible and worthy to attend higher education. The originator of the test himself, fought against tests being used as a standard in education.

There is a movement towards alternative schools and home schooling because once you hit 'the real world,' a lot of what was valued in school isn't valued out of school. You have to almost unlearn what you have spent over twelve years learning. This is explored in more depth in our chapter titled: "More Than A Fighting Chance."

What if children of all ages were taught to approach the things they need to do in life with how their younger selves would have approached it: with a curious and mysterious nature? Expect to fall, bang into things, get frustrated and have to do it again. Get people around you that will cheer for you, as opposed to telling you that you can't do it. Get people around you that will offer a hand as opposed to push you down. Put on your own protective gear to lessen the hurt from the falls and bangs instead of completely relying on others. What miss take are you going to take on today? Who are you going to invite to be with you on that path? If it's not happening at school make sure it's happening at home. By your reactions to test marks and through discussions about the traditional ways of learning that are taught at school, talk about a different mindset with your children. Don't let your child give up!

What Do I Want To Be When I Give Up

Along with the 'outlook-file' of "What Do I Want to be When I Give Up?" there is another 'outlook-file' that has been 'downloaded' by school: "All Things That Can, Go Wrong!" Think back to when you were a kid before you got those 'files.'

Remember When You Learned To Ride Your Bike

Think back to the joy and freedom you felt being in the moment of learning something new where you felt fully supported. You probably don't remember learning how to walk, but what about when you learned to ride a bike?

It's a beautiful thing when kids are learning to ride their bike. They ride into trees, parked cars, fire hydrants, hydro boxes and sometimes even people. It's a process. Nobody tells them they are wrong, dumb or can't do it. Instead, they are encouraged to keep doing and being; that they are to learn from their miss takes. The moment they ride without anyone's help is pure exhilaration! As they get older, there are more and more perks to riding their bike successfully; like riding to the neighbourhood park. As they get even older, to the corner store to get a special treat. (Guess what money they used to buy their special treat? If you guessed their allowance, you are right! Remember to use the chapter titled: "Setting Up Your Household For Success" to figure out how to give your child a way to earn allowance.) Then as they get even older, they may take their bike to a friend's house for a sleepover.

What Learning How To Ride A Bike Teaches Us

Let's treat kids in school as though they are learning how to ride a bike. Imagine the following as you get your math test back:

- It has a "C" on it with a happy face. Yes, a happy face! Just like when you were riding your bike and you fell, there were smiles because you were trying.

- When your teacher hands it back, she makes sure you are okay. Just like when you fell off your bike, people made sure you were okay.

- She tells you that she's happy that you did your best and that she's super excited to work with you on your corrections. Just like your parents, when you rode into the fire hydrant but you got back up to try again and corrected whatever it was that made you fall.

- She's super excited that your love for math is still there and she reminds you that it's just one test. Just like your parents when they wanted to instill a love for biking, so they told you that once you rode your bike you could get to the park in two minutes instead of the twenty it would take to walk.

- Then she tells you that she's super excited you will keep working hard in math because math is a muscle and a skill just like anything else. It just requires practice. There is no magical math brain that exists; it's just pure effort and repetition. Just like your parents were just super excited you were willing to get back up on your bike again and try again and again and again!

- She also says, "Let's figure out what went wrong." And she helps you assess: Did you copy a number down wrong? Did you forget to carry a number? Did you not remember a formula? Do you need more time? Do you need a quieter environment? Or, do you have no idea what went wrong? In this way, next time you will have a frame of reference on how to do better. Just like a parent checks: Is the seat too high or are the handlebars too low? You find a solution and adjust what isn't working for you.

- The teacher also lets the class know that most of the class didn't do very well so she needs to take some responsibly and figure out a different way to teach the skill. Just like the parent who took the training wheels off before the child was ready, may have to put the training wheels back on for a while.

Imagine If

What if learning and trying meant success in school? What if we were graded, not on the actual 'right' answer, but on the effort towards achieving the right answer? What if we were graded on the ability to come back from a failed attempt? What if we were graded on the ability to link subjects with our passions? What if we were graded on our ability to make connections between what we were learning in school and our lives? What if we were graded on our ability to recognize what we did wrong and our efforts to correct that? What if we were graded on our ability to say, "I know what I don't know." "I don't understand." "I need help." "I followed the example in the textbook and the example you gave us, and I still don't understand." Imagine—our schools would be a place of not giving up and not having the file that we learned about in the last chapter that says: "Everything that can, goes wrong."

Perhaps one day we will change the system to seeing all children as though they are just learning to walk or new to bike riding. In the meantime, you need to model a different perspective on learning with your kids. When they bring a test home, you model the change that you would like the schools to start adopting.

A Child's Self-Worth Is Tied To Their Grades

The difficult part of grading systems could be that children earn status in school, and potentially in the rest of their world, depending on their school performance. If their grades are low, this could lead to feelings of failure and frustration, especially if they are officially told they are less skilled than their peers. This can be seen as their "ability self-concept" and expectation for personal success declines. We want to avoid this decline in self-confidence and motivation as it may lead students to avoid certain courses or to withdraw from school altogether.

See if your child shies away from activities in which they are unlikely to succeed at. Hesitancy to try new things can depend on the meaning the child attaches to failure. Remember the two different mindsets, growth and fixed? By treating failure as something that is fixed, a child will not see how they can be successful.

How do we avoid tearing down a child's self-confidence and keeping them continuingly engaged in school no matter what their grade? Ensure that you have open communication with your child about what a grade really is. Once this understanding is there, then you can have the conversation about the importance of that grade. Make sure that you are hearing what the child says in this conversation and why you are putting worth on a particular grade or subject. Also, be very clear that this is only one part of what makes up your child. They are not the letter "C" that they are getting in Math; they are so much more.

> *By treating failure as something that is fixed, a child will not see how they can be successful.*

Alternative Environments For Skill Acquisition

To offset the lesson that failure is not okay in school, as well as for your child's confidence, ensure that your child is in extracurricular activities that help them gain new skills. Ones that will have to be worked for and not already known upon starting the activity. For example, the first time a child goes to karate, they aren't being entered into a competition. They grow their skills with each session and the premise is about learning and trying your best. They learn that they can become more successful over time in an atmosphere where failure is okay. Such programs have the freedom to be run in such a way, compared to schools, that design settings that support skill acquisition without emphasizing differences in children's abilities and talents.

Challenging activities which require them to gain a new skill in an environment where failure is okay is great for their brain development too. Math exercises are great for strengthening a specific part of their brain but overall challenging activities strengthen the entire networks in their brain.

Continuing To Embrace Miss Takes

Let's embrace the miss takes that our children make, as well as when they fail. Johnny is getting a "C" and we are quite upset about that. Meanwhile, Ms. Author Lady (yes, I'm talking about myself) is really 'twisted,' suggesting that's okay. I'm also pushing it one step further, suggesting that not only is a "C" okay but so is a failing mark.

I want to invite you to remember when your child was just learning how to walk. Also, remember back to when we used this analogy in our section titled: *"Our Success…With A*

Twist Success System" when we were explaining the clapperboard icon. I'm sure Johnny failed a lot of times and I'm sure you embraced, applauded and even cheered on his miss takes. I'm sure you even encouraged him to get up and try again. You may have even clapped when he fell because it means he was trying. You more than likely praised him for his ability to use a support like the table or a stool. You probably even gave him an aid, such as a walker, to help him. I'm sure there were times where you had to pick him up when he fell. And you didn't scold him for not getting it right the first 50 times. Or tell him that he wasn't doing it 'right' because he didn't do it like his older sibling.

Think of this as a movie you are shooting: "The Adventures of Johnny Learning to Walk!" All the times he tries, are the different takes: Take 1, Johnny tries to walk all the way, to Take 101, when he actually gets it. Hence, in our Signature Success System, changing the spelling of mistakes to miss takes. There were a lot of miss takes along the way when Johnny was learning to walk. If we didn't learn to walk until adulthood, how many adults would still be crawling? Probably most.

The simple fact is that Johnny took a test and failed.

The System Is Set Up For Perfection

Would you agree that every child goes into school wanting to be successful? Yet, the system is primarily set up for perfection, and not for learning from miss takes. Shouldn't school be looked at in its entire sum, be that a year at a time or for the potential eighteen or so years you could be in school? So, it's "The Adventures in the Educational Life of Johnny" as opposed to, "The Adventures in Grade Two, First Report Card, When My Child Got A "C.""

To recap from our chapter titled: "Liking The Child You Love," remember, what we feed, grows. Think of a flower: when it doesn't bloom, we don't put the blame on the flower or focus our energies on trying to fix the flower. We look at the environment the flower is in and see if it's receiving what it needs to grow and flourish. Let's do the same for our kids. One of the ways that we can do this is to engage in parent-teacher conferences and get a solid understanding of our child's environment.

> *To raise a success-ready child, you will need to ensure that you are focused daily on seeing your child through the 'growth lens'.*

Foundational Skills

Let's take a look at the child that didn't learn their multiplication tables in the early elementary school years. This foundational piece of math carries all the way through school. We often see children who feel that they are incapable of doing math. This could have come from a failed test, teachers' comments, other students' comments, and/or a comparison with siblings/friends.

One child may learn to ride a bike quickly with training wheels, another without training wheels. Some children may take longer to learn or fall off several times. Some may learn on a city street and others on a trail. The desired end result is the same: for a child to be able to pick up their bike and ride off, but the journey is different for every child.

With math, as an example, we would like each child to learn their multiplication tables, but where are the different accommodations for each child's journey? Rote learning–tests and worksheets—are not for everyone. But, welcome to our education system where rote learning, testing and worksheets comprise 95% of your child's learning.

More often than not, the child is not given the opportunity to go back to the basics since the curriculum just moves along. They are in Grade 3 so they should be learning the Grade 3 curriculum. If they don't do well, they couldn't possibly go back to the Grade 1 curriculum to see what gaps are missing, so the child loses confidence.

Teachers are aware that the grade they are teaching will have kids with the ability levels of two grades on either side. Grade 3 teachers should be aware that they can have a Grade 1 to Grade 5 range in different subjects. On top of that, one child could be at a Grade 5 level in Math and a Grade 2 level in English.

It would make sense to have three different groups of Math happening at the same time in this classroom: Grades 1 and 2 for those who need it, Grade 3 for kids who are exactly on their age target, and Grades 4 and 5 for those who are advanced.

In the twelve years I taught Grades 10 to 12, it amazed me the number of students that were sitting in my classes that were unable to write a simple paragraph, never mind an essay or research project. Who thought it was okay to pass them to that point in time? It shouldn't have been surprising, as the system keeps the same-aged students together, regardless of ability.

In the past ten years that I've been working with families, what we've come to learn is that not only is basic English not being accounted for, but the children we are seeing have no math sense and cannot recall simple addition or subtraction answers. Kids need, at the very least, these basic skills before heading into 'the real world.'

We don't fail kids until Grade 10. A child can conceivably get all the way to high school before there is a true awareness in the parents that their child doesn't understand basic Math and English. So now they are failing when it counts. But we don't fail them when it could grow them. Not surprisingly, the child just making the transition to high school, who is now failing his classes, loses even more confidence. The high school curriculum hasn't any time built in for going back to the basics to increase a child's confidence base, never mind checking for understanding.

Engagement In Learning

Have you noticed that your child comes home very rarely super excited about something being taught at school? Even when you ask them about what they learned that day, it's a sigh or "stuff" or my favourite answer, "nothing." But, the times they are excited to share with you is when it's related to something that they love or when the teacher is passionate about the subject.

My son had a teacher who taught him fractions using chocolate. He was pretty excited to share that story! Then at the end of the fraction unit, when she was sure they all understood it, they had pizza and divided it into fractions to eat. As my son loves both of those food groups, he remembers that years later.

Another teacher taught my child about Europe by using her own personal photos and stories. My child is still able to recite key facts about different places in Europe as she recalls the stories the teacher shared!

The best example of a teacher engaging their students and giving them a sense of hope in the system, in the combined seventeen years of my children's schooling, is a kindergarten teacher who listened to and observed the students' interests. At the beginning of the year, the children were into a certain craze for a toy called a Bayblade and the majority of the kids brought them in for Show and Tell and to play with at recess. She taught Math, letters, story time, etc. all by using the Bayblades. Next, they were really into Lego, so she switched to using Lego as the vehicle to teach the curriculum. It was amazing. The kids came home wanting to teach and share what they had learned because it tapped into an area of passion for them. Imagine teachers thinking that their primary responsibility is to teach students, not solely teach the curriculum as if it doesn't matter who is in front of them!

The next time your child suggests that they don't enjoy something they are learning, help them see where it fits in their life. For a child who doesn't like math but enjoys skateboarding, help them understand that it's all math-type principles which could help them become better skateboarders. Understanding angles, speed, and distance could give them an edge when doing skateboarding tricks! We can teach our kids to think of math as a means to an end. Learn math to help you be better at something you like by taking the knowledge learned and applying it to something you love.

A child that doesn't enjoy English but is passionate about movies could write movie critiques or scripts. Help them see that when they translate what they think about movies they watch into written form, then they can share their passion. Learning English and how to write well is a means to an end for communicating with the world. Since communication is super important for anything we do in life, let's change the way children look at English, from a stand-alone subject to a key foundational piece we need to live successfully.

If you are still saying that you really want your child to excel more in a given subject area, give them a reason to value it by making it relevant to their world. This may be something that you ask the school to help you with or search for resources on Google, YouTube or Facebook. Simply type into the search engine whatever their passion is with the subject they are struggling with. For example, "connections between dance and math." It's amazing what you can find!

At *Parenting…With A Twist*, we have used search engines to find amazing video's and resources that we have been able to share and use with the families we work with. Connect with us and we can also point you in the right direction. (Our contact information can be found at the end of each chapter in the "Parenting Skills Question" section.)

Age As The Requirement For School Placement

Children are grouped in school according to their age as of January 1st of the year they were born. This determines what grade they are put into across the board for every subject. So, all Grade 8's are on par in English, Math, Science, Social Sciences, Languages, Physical Education, etc.

As mentioned previously, not all students in a particular grade are on par which, if you remember, means a Grade 8 teacher will have kids ranging from Grade 6 to Grade 10. What if schools were organized by ability level, not simply by age? What amazingly strong learners we would have!

As that's not happening, you need to be aware of where your child falls on the continuum for the different subjects within their different grades. If your child is really advanced in math and finishes work before the rest of the kids, instead of getting bored, getting in trouble in class or always being made to help others out, why not use the math they have learned to create something? Or, have them find connections to what they learned and what they love? Or, why not have them advance by letting them go to a higher grade for math? Be aware and talk with your child's school about the solutions they can provide.

Parent-Teacher Interaction Specifically About Report Cards

As a teacher myself, as well as an engaged school parent, when my son's Grade 4 report card came home with the grades it had (you'll get full details below) I was in shock. It took me so off guard that I took pictures of the report card and texted them to my son's biological father, his bonus father and his maternal grandmother (also an educator) to see if I was missing something about my son. Each of those people that play a key role in my son's world had the same feeling of shock and we all came to the conclusion—we must have been given the wrong report card!

This experience taught me to more fully appreciate the experience that parents have who are not as well versed in the school system, either in terms of appropriate next steps to take or in deciphering what the grades actually mean. As a result, at Parenting…With A Twist, we offer our parents an opportunity to review school-based reports with them, as well as set up communication and attend key meetings so that the families feel supported and knowledgeable as their kids go through the system.

Treat School Like A Business

Think of the teacher like a business person you are dealing with. If you are in a school system in which your taxes pay the teacher salary, it really is like a business agreement. (Parents often reminded me of this fact when I was teaching in such a system, so just thought I'd pass that thought along.) Share what your expectations are for your child's education. If you aren't happy with the service you are receiving at a business, you would talk to them about your expectations. Treat the school system the same way. Tell them that you care more about your children's efforts, corrections, and passion for learning then you do about their marks. However, in understanding that the mark is important to the system, you need to see what they are using for assessments.

If you are feeling that your voice isn't being heard at the business, you call in the manager. In this case, you do the same thing, except it's the principal. The hope is that you are all on the same page and that they too want to ensure your child sees learning and school as something they are excited about in their lives.

We asked for a parent-teacher conference to receive more clarification about the marks and comments on the shocking report card mentioned above.

Invite Your Child's Cheerleaders

I asked the principal to also be a part of the meeting. The principal was well acquainted with my son as there had been School Team Based meetings for him every year. As you may recall from the chapter titled: "Please Do Label My Child," students who have official Individualized Education Plans (IEP) have School Team Based meetings so that all the key players at the school level, as well as the parents, are aware of and accountable for the accommodations stated in the IEP. My son did not have an official IEP, however, and you also may remember that I'm a big advocate of having a child labelled if that's what it takes to have them stand out as an individual.

My son had started to display anxiety-like behaviours in Grade 1 and each year we asked for an Education Plan to be put in place to support him. One of the accommodations in this plan was for my son to go to the principal's office if he was feeling anxious. The principal had special jobs for him to do, as well as a table that he could sit and play a game or do some work on. My son used this accommodation over the course of Grades 2 and 3 so he and the principal had built a relationship. While I wanted the principal to be apart of this meeting as the manager, I also wanted her to be there to be an advocate for my son. It's key to have your child surrounded by cheerleaders. This is discussed in detail in the chapter titled: "The Language of Leadership."

The Shocking Report Card

I am not a believer in marks defining my child. However, I was aware that this was the first time our son received a report card that conveyed his marks through letter grades and he had a certain expectation of what the letter grades would be. In the school system he's enrolled in, Grade 4 is the year where they introduce letters as grades as opposed to numbers.

Our son came racing in to open his report card with great expectation of these new-to-him letter grades! There was a comment about his reading "not being at grade level" and a "C" in Language Arts attached to that comment. There was a "B" in Mathematics and Physical Education. The Physical Education comment suggested he needed to "improve his soccer skills." There was also another "C" in Art. My son burst into tears when he saw that. That wasn't how he saw himself. As mentioned above, that wasn't how other key people in his life saw him either. At Parenting…With A Twist, we speak to families often in which a child has had great expectations on a mark for something, only to have their hopes dashed.

As we aren't a house that focuses on grades, I had to understand where his expectation of what his grades should be was coming from, as well as get clear on where comments about what an acceptable grade was or wasn't, was coming from. When we talked to our son, he suggested that there were signs all over the classroom of what the different letter grades meant and that it was talked about for weeks leading up to the report cards being given out. So, even in a household where grades aren't given much merit, the pressure from the school system in relation to grades was felt. Imagine the pressure your child is feeling if you put that much weight on grades at home as well.

As a family, we reminded our son of our thoughts on grades and the reasons why we believed that. That was helpful for him as it took some of the sting out of the marks. I must remind you, as parents, this also applies to the report card that is all top marks. Marks need to be looked at as what they are: a person's understanding of a particular concept in a particular subject at a given point in time–that's it.

At Parenting…With A Twist, we have had several families contact us that cannot understand how their child sailed through their elementary and high school years with top marks and then ended up flunking out of university. If we remember what a mark is and nothing more, that wouldn't be surprising. When we look at everything a mark is not telling us, we can understand that phenomenon.

We also told our son that while grades weren't the focus of what education was to us, that we were going to get curious with his teacher about the report. Why did we do this even though marks don't mean a lot to us? We wanted to examine the environment to see how we could help our son grow. We wanted his teacher to know we were his cheerleaders and that we saw him in a completely different light than the report card suggested. We wanted the teacher to realize that our son's engagement and growth needed to be as important to him as it was to us. We did not want our son to start asking himself the question: "What do I want to be when I give up?"

The Parent-Teacher Conference About The Shocking Report Card

In relation to the Language Arts mark, the teacher had never heard my son read, so he assumed he wasn't reading at grade level. As this was three months into the school year, it was a shock to us that the teacher hadn't heard him read. We showed the teacher the books he was reading: books from the Young Adult section of the library and the Harry Potter book that was in his desk at school. We asked the teacher what grade level he thought the books were. The teacher suggested about a Grade 8 reading level and we gently reminded him that our son was only in Grade 4. We asked him to make a point to read with Marley before the next report card so that he could make an informed decision about his grade as opposed to basing it on an assumption.

Make an A** Out of You and Me

Where could your child's teacher be making an assumption about something that is affecting their mark? Teachers, as humans, can and do make assumptions about a child, from how they dress, to the lunch they bring, to their behaviours. So, it's super important that we clarify any assumptions they could be making about our children, as we do know them better than the teachers do.

Employers may make similar assumptions about their employees. There was a study conducted that suggested that "good looking people" have a higher chance of getting a job after an initial interview than those deemed, by society, to be not as good looking. Assumptions are made everywhere. I used to have an overhead slide that said, "Who You Are Speaks So Loudly, I Can't Hear What You Are Saying!" This slide had a picture of a person dressed up as a clown. I would have a talk with my students about how looking and acting like a clown may change someone's opinion of you. Teachers and other key influencers in your child's world, as humans, will make assumptions too.

Using The Tools And Systems That Are In Place

Another component of the Language Arts mark was that my son didn't hand in two assignments on time. The teacher had the assignments at our meeting and told us that he would have graded them at a 3 out of 4 but, as there were late, they got a mark of zero.

I looked on the board where the teacher had a system laid out: he put a dot beside all assignments that were not handed in as a reminder for the students to hand them in. Great system, in theory. There was no dot beside our son's name. We reviewed our son's agenda and there was nothing in the daily communication between the teacher and ourselves that mentioned anything about late assignments. Neither my son, nor us as the parents, had knowledge that the assignments were late.

We asked if moving forward, the system the teacher had in place could be used more effectively. One step further, we asked him to have our son write in his agenda any outstanding assignments he had. This would help keep us in the know. Plus, it would teach our son that beyond an agenda being a communication tool, it could also be used to record things you need to remember to do. If you are going to set your child up for success, you have to teach them the tools to do so, and give them the practice to use those tools!

I mention this because we, too, made our own assumptions. We assumed that the teacher would be communicating with us through our son's planner. We signed the planner every day and wrote our notes to the teacher in it, and assumed the teacher would be doing the same. It is important to be clear on what you want in relation to your child, with their key influencers.

The Intentional Reduction Of A Mark

The "B" in Math was surprising. In Grades 2 and 3, by about the third week of school, our son's teachers had asked if they could give him more challenging work as he was understanding the Math lessons without much explanation. We knew that he had been a very strong Math student. From September of that school year to the first report card in December, our son had also shared with us that he achieved 100% and 97% on his two Math tests and 87% on his Math quiz.

It turns out that the teacher reduced his mark intentionally. In early September, my son had been away from school for two days and missed some class work. As a result of that missed work the teacher dropped his mark to a "B." This was to show my son how important seat work is.

There was no recognition that my son was doing extremely well, even with missed seat work, and as with the Language Arts missing work, there was no communication to indicate to either myself or my son that this work was missing. We asked if moving forward, we could receive this type of communication for all subjects. Again, in not wanting to make any assumptions, we clearly asked for Math to be included in all agenda communications.

What If Your Child Is Bored

Another piece of information that came up was that our son was completing his Math seat work ahead of the other kids. He was, then, reading during Math class work time and asking us, his parents, if he could miss school, suggesting that he was bored and ahead in class. I asked the teacher if our son could be given something more challenging to do. If I was taking my own advice, I would have asked if he could go to the next grade for the Math portion of the day. As we explored earlier in this book, there are students up to two grades below and above the actual grade level their age dictates them to be in.

Typically, teachers want the kids who are finished first to help the other kids. This is fine in moderation, but you also want to keep your child engaged and challenged.

I mention this as children often get in trouble in class for being unfocussed or wasting time. What if they are acting in such a way because they find the work too easy or too hard or they aren't having breakfast every morning? Keeping the lines of communication open with your child's key influencers, in this case their teacher, enables the teacher to better understand your child and their needs. More time will be spent on the importance of key influencers and how to identify who they are in your child's world in the chapter titled: "The Language of Leadership."

Who Have You Been Teaching For Three Months

The "B" in Physical Education (P.E.) was surprising, especially with the accompanying comment: "Needs to develop his soccer skills." Our son has played academy soccer from the age of four. I hope you are beginning to see just how shocking these marks and comments were to us. This comment really solidified our thought that we had just gotten the wrong person's report card.

We asked about how the P.E. mark was assessed. The teacher had chosen ONE day during the THREE months of soccer skills training to assess the students' abilities. In doing this assessment, he genuinely felt my son didn't have very good soccer skills. So again, we had to remind our son what a mark is, say it with me: a person's demonstration of their understanding of a particular concept in a particular subject at a given point in time.

The teacher had no idea he was a soccer player—this solidifies my point that, quite often teachers are so focused on teaching the curriculum, they aren't getting to know who's in front of them.

Keep Your Child's Creativity Alive

With our son suggesting that the "C" in Art meant that he couldn't draw, we really wanted this addressed so that we could keep his creativity alive. So, again, we wanted to see what the teacher was basing this on. The teacher showed us a drawing that he gave the class as an example of "line art" then showed us our son's and another student's. Our son's line art did not look exactly like the example and the other student's did. So, he was given a 2 out of 4 and the other child was given a 4 out of 4. So 'art' in this teacher's mind, was to copy exactly what the teacher had shown the class.

Where does your child let their mark define their abilities? My son used to love to draw and had never uttered the words that he couldn't do it. We weren't going to let our child be defined by the "C" he received. The mark he got in this case was subjective—it was based on his teacher's definition of art.

To further drive this point home, we took him to an art gallery and we had him critique the work. This experience helped him to understand that art, like many things in life, is really subjective. What a life lesson to receive in Grade 4!

What Mark Would I Get If I Handed This In As Is

We asked, if moving forward, our son could show his work to the teacher and ask, "What mark would this piece receive if I was to hand it in as is?" Then, he could decide if he wanted to add to what he was handing in or leave it as it was. In essence, he was in control of his mark. It was important for him to understand that the sooner he knew he was behind, the easier it would be to catch up.

Be The Helicopter When You Need To Be

The teacher had taken no opportunity in three months to discuss any of what he perceived the issues to be. Even though the teacher saw me on a regular basis as I was active in my son's classroom a minimum of once a week. Also, even with having a School Based Team meeting and a one-to-one meeting with detailed notes in relation to my son's anxiety-like behaviours. Another assumption made on my part was that the teacher would have approached me with concerns as opposed to waiting for the report card to share his thoughts. In not wanting to be the "helicopter parent," after having the two meetings that were standard, I didn't ask him if there was anything I should be aware of. The term "helicopter parent" was first used in Dr. Haim Ginott's 1969 book Parents & Teenagers by teens who said their parents would hover over them like a helicopter. Helicopter parents typically take too much responsibility for their children's experiences and, specifically, their successes or failures.

I've learned that as parents it's okay that we do quick check-ins. As a business owner, I've since changed our policies in regards to communication with parents. At Parenting…With A Twist, we have always given our families a Monthly Report at the beginning of each month for what we covered with them in the preceding month. Following what occurred with my son's teacher, we added a column to the report titled, "Parental Support" to enable our team members to officially report to parents what we need their help with at home to further support their children. This was added with the understanding that we will not wait the entire month to let them know something that could be helpful immediately. For instance, if we noticed that a student of ours was enjoying reading a particular genre of book with us, we would note that in the report but also tell the parent right away so they could start reading those types of books with their child as well.

Specific Parent-Teacher Conference Questions

If it's important to you to see your child's mark change, then you need to not only have a conference with the teacher but also ask some very specific questions. I've included those questions in detail below. The "you" in these questions refers to the teacher. The "you" in the explanation below the question refers to you as the parent. Please contact us if you'd like a copy of these questions. (Our contact information can be found at the end of each chapter in the "Parenting Skills Question" section.)

1. "Can you explain the breakdown of my child's current mark?"
-You will want to ensure that you are being honest about where your child is at in their home life as well. This helps the teacher see your child as a whole, rather than just a mark.

2. "What do you see are my child's weaknesses and strengths?"
-Having the growth mindset, you will want to see weaknesses as correctable and strengths as the effects of hard work.

3. "Can you please show me the assessment criteria you used to mark my child's work?"
- This is important as it lets you know what the teacher was looking for when assigning marks, particularly for report cards.

4. "Was my child aware of this criteria prior to completing the work?"
-If not, you will want this to change. Your child must be aware of what they are getting marked on prior to handing in their work. Otherwise, it's like telling a child you are going to rate how well they ride their bike but you haven't told them that you expect them to jump two curbs and pop a wheely!

5. "How many pieces of work were assessed?"
-Your child might have received a "C" on one assignment and that defined their whole mark. Then you will have to decide if the mark is really worth stressing over as one test is not an accurate representation of your child's abilities.

6. "Can you please show me the work that was assessed and the assessment sheet that assigned my child their mark?"
-This will let you know what was actually included in determining the mark, as well as see where your child is falling short.

7. "Did my child have an opportunity to practice the skill before being marked on it? If so, can you please show me their work from inception to completion?"
-This will let you see the process the teacher worked through with your child to learn the skill being assessed, as well as your child's progress on the journey.

8. "Did my child have an opportunity to re-hand in any of the work or can they still re-hand in work?"
-Now that you and your child know what the expectations are, determine how they could improve.

9. "Can you please show me what an "A" assignment looks like for the assignments that my child did not do well on?"
-This will give you an idea of that specific teacher's expectations.

10. "Can I please have any upcoming assessment criteria and assignment due dates and topics?"
-This information will be needed so you can fully support your child in any assessment pieces, moving forward.

11. "Can you please provide me with the upcoming schedule of all student work: topics, assignments, tests?"
-You will be able to help your child prepare more effectively using the "Reverse Homework" method discussed in the chapter titled: "The Dog Ate My Homework & Study Notes."

12. "Can you set up a dialogue between my child and yourself, where they show their piece that will be assessed and have you determine what grade level it is currently?"
-This gives your child responsibility in the process and allows them to make a conscious choice to improve and understand how to do so.

13. a) "Will you provide any sort of review for the final exam (if there is one)?"
-Getting a review for the final exam ensures that your child is aware of what is on it. When your child does the review, they will see if they understand the material. Remember to have your child put the dates for final exams in their agenda and then work backwards from that date to put in when they should study, when they should have the review completed by, and when they should schedule time for asking the teacher any questions they don't understand.

b) "If so, can my child have the review earlier?"
-It's important to get the review as soon as the teacher is able to provide it as that gives your child more time to manage all the tasks that go into writing an exam.

c) "If not, what could you suggest my child do to prepare?"
-When a teacher doesn't provide a review, this makes it heard on the student to know what the important pieces are that they have covered.

14. "What would be the best course of action right now to catch up, keep up, and/or excel?"
-The teacher ultimately decides on the grade your child is going to get, as well as the path it will take them to get there; so, it's best to make an action plan for success with them.

15. "How is it best to communicate with you moving forward?"
-Agenda, email, phone call, and/or in person meetings could be some of the suggestions.

16. "Are you willing to communicate with a tutor?"
-If so, ask them what the best method of communication would be.

Blind Acceptance

Sixteen pretty detailed questions. Why? From the perspective of a parent, teacher, tutor, and employer (I play all of those roles) you want to know how your child is being assessed and understand how to help your child see that a grade is something that can be changed. This is a growth mindset. This is looking at the environment to see how to make your child grow. And this is teaching your child that there is a process involved in improving or changing something.

Where might a key influencer have a subjective definition of something and judge your child based on that? A coach may believe that arriving late means you shouldn't have equal play time. If this isn't in the league rules, then it's a subjective rule. A child or parent would then have the right to question this by presenting a different take on that rule. Be aware of where your child can learn to question the way something is, as opposed to blind acceptance.

Parenting Skills Questions

Amber Highlighted Stop Sign: Use Caution When Proceeding
How do you role model this? Role modelling is a way of signalling what's appropriate in terms of how you behave, what you do, the activities you engage in, and what you believe. Remember to share these answers with your Accountability Partner!

Circles: Different Lenses We Put On

1. Your friend is upset that their child got a mark they feel is unacceptable.

a) List what you could talk to her about, with what you now know about marks, to help her understand what a mark actually measures.

b) Tell her what she can do to affect positive change in her child's mark.

c) Tell her what she can do to help her child's self-worth.

2. Have a conversation with your child about:

a) what tests measure and don't measure;

b) how you will view marks moving forward.

3. How can you link your child's passion to their schooling?

4. How can you help your child re-engage in school?

5. a) Give an example of something your child didn't do as well in as you thought they could.

b) Did you look at it through a growth or a fixed mindset?

c) If you looked at it with a fixed mindset, have a conversation with your child now about it, through the growth mindset.

Clapperboard: Miss Take versus Mistake & A.C.T. (Action Changes Things)

6. a) Besides school grades, what else can you tie your child's self worth to?

b) Why is it good for children to be exposed to extracurricular opportunities?

7. a) When is the last time you took up something new?

b) Did you get it the first time you tried it?

c) What did it feel like to fail?

8. a) Have you ever given up on something because you were afraid of failure?

b) What is something you would try if you knew you couldn't fail?

9. a) Describe three situations that you had at school or that your child has faced where it would be appropriate to use the following sentences: "I know what I don't know." "I don't understand." "I need help." "I followed the example in the textbook and the example you gave us, and I still don't understand."

b) Have your child practice these statements with you.

Heart: Life Experiences that Shape Us

10. Share your answers to #7 and #8 with your child.

11. Think of a time that your child successfully learned a new skill that took them some time to get it and you had a growth mindset. (As we've used throughout this book, for most families, walking or bike riding are two examples.)

a) What was your belief in them learning this new skill?

b) Find a photograph of them learning this skill. If you don't have one, create an image that represents this.

c) Share this photograph/image with your child.

d) Put this photograph/image where you and your child will see it on a daily basis to remind you both that miss takes and failure are a part of life.

Target: S.M.A.R.T. Goal Setting System

12. Arrange an initial conversation with your child's teacher to discuss:

a) The assessment practices used this year. (You want to ensure that there are a variety of assessments pieces being used, not only tests.)

b) The best method of communication for both of you.

c) Expectations of when this communication will happen and what you will be focussing on.

13. Arrange a secondary conversation with your child's teacher to discuss:

a) What grade level your child is at in their core subjects of reading, writing, comprehension, and mathematics and why they are suggesting that.

b) What the teacher will be doing with your child to reduce their deficiencies and capitalize on their strengths.

14. If the teacher is unsure of what grade level your child is at in the core subjects, please reach out to us and we will give you the tools to determine your child's level and suggestions of how to support them.

15. Arrange a third conversation with your child's teacher to discuss:

a) Work that was assessed by the teacher and that was not given an acceptable mark, by your house standards.

b) Prior to the conversation with the teacher: Applaud your child for the mark and the effort they put into it. Ask them what their perspective is on the mark they received. Explain to your child why this particular mark is important to you and why you feel it's important to them. Suggest that to make an improvement on something that is being assessed by a particular individual, in this case the teacher, that a conversation with the individual needs to happen in order to see improvements.

c) In the conversation with the teacher: Glean what the teacher's perspective was as to why this mark was given. How, as a team, the mark can be improved on this particular assessed work. How, moving forward, your child's perspective and the teacher's perspective can be accounted for.

We are invested in your success, so please remember to connect with us if you run into any difficulties or need any help with these questions.

You can connect with us at our *Parenting… With A Twist* Facebook page at Facebook.com/parentingwithatwist, or click to parentingwithatwist.com

*"Motivation is what gets you started.
Habit is what keeps you going."*

\- Jim Rohn

Parenting Tip #8
The Dog Ate My Homework And My Study Notes

The Necessity of Homework

According to the National Centre for Education Statistics, the average high school day is 6.7 hours long. The average child has 3.5 hours of homework per night, according to Education Week. That's a 10-hour day—every day. On top of this is any extracurricular activities a student may have.

There is a raging debate about whether homework is necessary for kids to learn. I don't believe that kids need copious amounts of homework. They do need homework to help them understand that when you work towards a goal, you need to put structured time aside to do so. In the traditional public school system here isn't a class called, "Homework 101" where how to do homework is taught, never mind how to do homework if you are not a read/write learner.

Homework teaches children how to take responsibility for tasks and how to work independently. Homework helps children develop mental habits that will serve them well as they proceed through school and, indeed, through life. Planning and organizing tasks, managing time, making good choices, and problem solving—all skills that contribute to effective functioning in the adult world.

Homework is not meant to actually teach a child the lessons from that day but more to reinforce good habits. This is an important distinction. Be aware if your child is consistently coming home with topics they haven't been taught, yet are expected to bring their work back to school completed. This would involve a conversation with the teacher if it becomes a pattern.

Often times, we hear that work is not corrected or checked for understanding, but only for completion. Then they are tested and everybody is surprised when the student who got a perfect mark on their homework, doesn't do well on the test. This is another reason why grades do not define intelligence. Completed work doesn't automatically equal understanding. If you learn that your child is regularly not doing well on their tests but is getting near perfect on their classwork and/or homework, get curious with the teacher. Is the classwork/homework being marked for accuracy and understanding? If so, then why is your child not doing well on their tests? Do they have a fear around tests or are the tests not on what was in the class/homework? If not, then how is your child supposed to know what they don't know?

The amount of work your child is bringing home needs to seem reasonable. The standard recommendations, as set by the National Parent Teacher Association in the United States and used by the Canadian school boards I've worked in, are: 10-20 minutes per night in the first grade and an additional 10 minutes per grade level thereafter (e.g., 20 minutes for second grade, 120 minutes for twelfth). High school students may sometimes do more, depending on what classes they take.

Have a conversation with the teacher as to how these guidelines can be tailored to your child. In a previous chapter, I indicated that if a child had a formal assessment done by a psychologist, they had a legal right to get an Individualized Education Plan set up for them at school that would state accommodations for them. For example, the Plan might suggest that a child only do two questions for every math concept instead of all the math questions dealing with the same concept found in that particular section of the math textbook. There is no reason that you couldn't ask the classroom teacher for your child to be given the same accommodation.

If your child is bringing homework they didn't complete during class time, as opposed to work that was assigned to do at home, you will want to explore why that's happening in the classroom. Then, come up with some school-based solutions with your child and their teacher, as classwork should not be homework.

If a child, who has been sitting all day, now has to go home and sit to do more school work, that might cause a rebellion. If they don't see the value in what they are learning, they might not have a purpose or a reason to do the work. Never fear, we have solutions here.

Confidence & Self-Management, Please
Every single parent we've ever met with identifies 'confidence' as THE number one goal for their child. Chances are, a child will be more confident if the child understands the teacher. So again, a parent and child want the same thing!!

Parent: "I would like my child to have more confidence."

Child: "I would like to understand what the teacher is saying."

Parenting…With A Twist Coach: "Let's solve this situation together!"

This leads to a series of questions:

- When did the child first start not understanding?

- Has anybody ever made them feel that they just aren't going to understand it, no matter what they try?

- Are they defined by the last mark they got?

- Do they feel challenged?

- Is there a pattern to them not understanding?

- Do they see a connection between what they are learning in school and in other parts of their life?

- Do they embrace their miss takes and know that failing is okay?

And the list goes on!

Now, envision what you want for your child and what they want for themselves and work toward this vision, understanding that there will be miss takes along the way that will lead to the shared vision. We will use one of our most common examples: homework being a fight. Let's look at what each party might desire to happen.

Parent's Vision: "A confident child that pulls out their agenda and their school work and completes it at the kitchen table, occasionally asking for my input."

Child's Vision: "I take out my work and everything I need to complete the work, as I know I can do the work, and I understand the expectations of both my teacher(s) and my parents. My parent trusts that I will get this work done by its due date."

While we understand the desire, now we have to understand that there are actions that will get us to it. With these actions, there will be miss takes made along the way to achieving the vision of what you both want! Remember it's just a 'take' in the process to get there! Just as your child had to learn how to walk, there is a process in how to do school work!

Your children will have to learn how to:

- use an agenda,

- understand different teachers' expectations,

- understand different parents' expectations,

- understand what their school work is asking,

- understand how to do the school work,

- know what to do when they don't know how to do the school work,

- understand what their best environment is to complete the work,

- know what tools they need to complete the school work,

- know how to regulate themself to sit down and do the work,

- understand time management to get the work completed in a timely fashion,

- understand why the school work is relevant to their life,

- find a connection between their work and their interests,

- know how they learn so that they aren't just doing the work for the sake of doing the work but to actually retain and learn from it.

Take 1 to Take 1,001 Versus "Just Do It"

And here you were thinking that in relation to homework, your child just needs to 'do it!' Imagine if you just plunked your child down one day and thought walking should have been that easy.

Now you understand that there is going to be a 'Take 1' to a 'Take 1001' to get to the goal! In order to make the end result happen, we have to look at the other factors (i.e. media time, food intake, co-parenting, confidence, and the list goes on). But, just like shooting a movie, there are many takes—to adjust the lighting, the music, the script, the costumes etc.—for the take to finally be right. Your child and you are worth all the takes it takes to get there!

Let's stop and think for a second of the language used in the making of a movie. They say: "Act 1, Scene 1." I'd like you to think of the acronym ACT (Action Changes Things).

Learning Styles & Homework

Tonight, Jenny has to learn her times tables, practice spelling words, and write a paragraph using her spelling words. When her older sibling had to do this, you were able to cook dinner while holding up flash cards, calling out the spelling list, and then the paragraph would 'just get done.'

What you didn't know was that the older sibling is a read-write learner, a people pleaser, received a compliment on her work today at school, ate her whole lunch and had a healthy snack after school. Now you do the same process with Jenny thinking that it will be as easy as it was with her sister! Nope—Jenny has no desire to follow the same process as her older sibling. You label Jenny as the "problem child" who is nothing like her older sister, who loves school and 'just does well.'

What you don't know is that Jenny is a kinesthetic learner. For a kinesthetic learner, who just sat for most of the day at school, to then have to sit down again to do homework is torture! What would enhance Jenny's learning? Doing her times tables while she's bouncing on the trampoline, kicking a soccer ball or shooting hoops. Instead of rewriting her spelling words on a piece of paper, she'd like to trace them in shaving cream or sand. And if at the end of a very long school day you still expect her to sit to write something, she'd like to do it on a yoga ball. Kinesthetic learners need movement and something hands-on to retain information. To take a test to see what Kind of Learner you and your child are, please contact us. (Our contact information can be found at the end of each chapter in the "Parenting Skills Question" section.)

Also, because Jenny has to sit for most of the day in school, at lunch, when she's supposed to be eating, she's too busy walking around. After school, she races home to drop her bag off and heads off to play! Since breakfast, she's eaten about half a sandwich. When she jumped up in excitement in class when the recess bell went, she got in trouble and had to miss five minutes of recess. As it's been so frustrating doing her times tables at night, she didn't know the answers when the teacher randomly called on her in class. But, hey, Jenny should 'just do it' like her older sister did!

Studying 101

Just like homework, your child might not be taught how to study effectively either. And what are the majority of marks made up of? Test results. And there isn't a class at most traditional, public high schools called "Studying 101" yet children are expected to be able to know how to study.

How are children expected to study? It's typically the same way they are taught. If they have been taught by a textbook and question/answer, they will usually use their textbook and questions/answers to study. This is great for read/write learners as the information is more likely to have already stuck for them. It's not so great for the other learners as it doesn't accommodate the way their brains work. So it's yet another school piece in which the majority of learners don't feel successful. Remember the file in our brain: "What do we want to be when we give up?" We are getting more and more clarity as to why that is!

Studying & Time Management

The announcement of a test would be a great time to learn time management/project management. This is a skill that Google resources claim is more important than top marks when hiring someone. Imagine if teachers suggested to their students to write when the test is scheduled for in their agenda.

The only time my children have used their agendas is with their Elementary teacher and it has been to copy down something that their teacher has written on the board. It typically involves what happened that day or what is happening the next day, not to plan for something in the future.

Let's teach our children to use the agenda as a time/project management tool. Let's say the test is for Science, Chapters 5, 6 and 7, and it is on December 6th. The teacher would tell the students to flip to the date in their agenda and they would go to December 6th and write "Science Test: Chapters 5, 6 & 7."

- Then, the day before, (Dec. 5th) they would write: "Block time off for studying for Science Test."

- Then, two days before, (Dec. 4th) they would write: "Block time off for studying for Science Test."

- Then, three days before, (Dec. 3rd) they would write in their agenda: "Ask any questions you still have for Science Test."

- Then, four days before, (Dec. 2) they would write in their agenda: "Highlight questions/concepts that I don't understand for Science Test."

- Then, five days before, (Dec 1st) they would write in their agenda: "Review Chapter 7."

- Then, six days before, (Nov 30th) they would write in their agenda: "Review Chapter 6."

- Then, seven days before, (Nov 29th) they would write in their agenda: "Review Chapter 5."

Studying & Learning Styles

Plus, the way each child, for their predominant learning style, should study would be explained so that they don't go home thinking they will just read their textbook and notebook over and cross their fingers that the information is retained.

If your teacher is not doing either of the above approaches with your child, I invite you to do both.

Since you've discovered how your child learns (remember our chapter titled: "Please Label My Child") you will want to dig a littler deeper to find out how someone with that learning style should study and do their homework. For example, let's say everybody from the same science class went home with their notes and needed to review them. A visual learner would want to highlight the key points and/or turn the key words into pictures. An auditory learner would want to take the key points and make it into a song and/or have a discussion with someone about this learning. A kinesthetic learner would love to be sitting on a yoga ball or jumping on a trampoline while they review notes and/or find examples of how that information relates to their life. A read/write learner can summarize their notes in the side margin through the use of bullet points and will most likely prefer a quiet place to do this in. Reach out to us and ask us to send you the PDF we have created that provides more details as to how to do homework and study based on one's predominant learning style. (Our contact information can be found at the end of each chapter in the "Parenting Skills Question" section.)

Teach your child how to use their agenda. Teach them executive life skills by being an amazing manager of time and projects!

Imagine how confident your children will be in the 'real world' with this talent mastered. As you do this exercise with them, you may even see your own ability to manage time and projects improve.

Reverse Homework

Another solution, which appeals to all children's learning styles, is to give a child pre-knowledge of the material in a format that works for their brain. Let's say the science teacher gives the topic of the human Digestive System to his students before he actually teaches it to them. He wants them to preview the material so that when they hear about it in class, it's not the first time. When you've heard something before, you have a comfort level of familiarity when you hear it again. At Parenting…With A Twist, we refer to this as reverse homework.

For the read/write learner to preview the Digestive System, they are given information to read along with questions and answers. They are to bring the answered questions to class. For the visual learners, they are given a diagram to digest (ha ha!) They are to replicate the drawing and bring it to class. For the auditory learners, they are given a link to a video where the parts of the digestive system are rapped to a popular tune. They can either rap it to the class or explain it. For the kinesthetic learners, they are given a link to a video to watch which shows a doctor dissecting the digestive system. They are to act out the dissection.

Imagine your child walking into class with some knowledge and understanding of the lesson, instead of feeling totally overwhelmed. Their confidence would soar. Next imagine that they knew that they weren't expected to understand it immediately, which often is the pressure felt in class. Further imagine, it's taught to them in a way that fires up their brain, not only by how the textbook or classroom teacher teaches it. Lastly, imagine how they would feel knowing it was expected there would be questions on the material they could ask the teacher — that it would be okay to not understand! The number one wish from parents for their kids that we work with is that the kids feel more confident with how they learn, with the material, and with asking for help.

There are schools that do this reverse homework method and have experienced great success. Schools that have adopted this idea in the United States saw their failure rate drop from 35% to 10% and saw their college enrolment up from 63% to 80% in two years.

While the students preview the topic at home, class time is spent on answering the kids' questions about the material, working through applying the information to real-world situations, and finding links with the subject material and their passions. Reverse homework get kids engaged in their learning and develops a sense of responsibility because the students feel there is value in doing the work. Parents are happy as they see their children's confidence soar. Since our team at *Parenting…With A Twist* discovered this homework concept, we've been introducing it to all of our families and coaching them on how to best use it.

If your child's school is not using the reverse homework method, you can advocate for your child to have access to the teacher's plan for the school year. This plan is submitted by the teacher to the administration and outlines when they will be covering the different curriculum expectations they are required to teach. By getting this teaching plan you will have the upcoming topics. Once you know your child's learning style, you will be able to have them do a reverse homework activity on the upcoming topics. You can go to the library or into Google for resources. Remember, it's okay to not have all the answers as long as you are willing to and know how to access help.

What if your son is well versed in how he learns and can confidentially use the tools needed to successfully learn and retain the information taught? What if his learning style is accommodated in class? Imagine the difference it would make. In our experience, families well versed in this information experience success in school and life!

Parenting Skills Questions

Does this sound familiar?

Parent: "I would like my child to do their work without a fight."

Child: "I would like to be able to do my work without my parents nagging me."

Notice they have the same goal!

Amber Highlighted Stop Sign: Use Caution When Proceeding

How do you role model this? Role modelling is a way of signalling what's appropriate in terms of how you behave, what you do, the activities you engage in, and what you believe. Remember to share these answers with your Accountability Partner!

Circles: Different Lenses We Put On

1. The next time your child has homework and it's an issue, ask these questions:

-Do they understand the work?

-Do they have an example to follow?

-Do they know how to do the work?

-Do they have the tools to do the work?

-Do they know when it's due?

-Do they have the assignment?

-Do they know how to get started?

-Do they have the right physical space to do their homework?

-Do they understand why they need to do their homework?

-Do they value homework?

Clapperboard: Miss Take versus Mistake & A.C.T. (Action Changes Things)

2. Show them that they need homework in order to develop the habit that highly successful people have. As suggested, homework is simply putting structured time aside to work towards a goal. Help them understand that when they are working towards a goal, they need to put structured time aside to do so. This means that you, as the parent, need to set some time aside to do work that needs to be done on a regular basis and call it your homework.

a) Write a list of things you could do that could be considered your homework (grocery list, budgeting, tax receipts, bills, this book etc.)

b) Start scheduling time to do this work. (Hint: alongside your child would be ideal.)

3. Is the homework they are bringing home consistently on topics they haven't been taught, yet are expected to bring their work back to school completed? If so, please reach out to the teacher to ensure they know that approach is not acceptable to you.

4. Use these next points as a checklist to ensure the following is in place in your home for your child (and now you) to have a successful homework experience:

a) It's very important, within your home, to have a designated place for school items as this develops structure for homework completion. Do you have this set up?

b) You will also want to make sure all the necessary school supplies and tools are handy.

c) Kids need to understand that there is a greater reason for homework, such as the life skill of self-discipline that can only be developed with practice. Where is your child's lack of motivation coming from?

d) Assess the homework environment to ensure that your child has the right atmosphere to work in. Is it distraction free? Is your child full of good energy from a snack/water?

(Section continued on next page.)

Clapperboard: Miss Take versus Mistake & A.C.T. (Action Changes Things), continued

e) Pay careful attention if resistance happens only with one subject or across all subjects. Examine this further.

f) If it's a bigger assignment, is there a possibility to do homework in pieces, instead of all at once? Or if it's a set of questions that all deal with the same concept, then how about having them do all the even or odd ones, instead of all of them?

g) It can be very frustrating to be a kinesthetic learner then have to sit and do worksheets after being in a chair for most of the day at school. Explore with your child how they learn (as we've talked about in a previous chapter.) Use this information as a tool to talk with your child and their teacher so that you can set them up for homework success.

h) Children listen more to our behaviour than our words, so don't forget to do some homework alongside them.

i) Please contact us if you would like a copy of a HOMEWORK Checklist PDF that we designed so you can assess your homework situation and figure out how to improve it. (Our contact information can be found at the end of each chapter in the "Parenting Skills Question" section.)

Target: S.M.A.R.T. Goal Setting System

5. How can you implement "reverse homework" at your house?

6. Is the homework your child brings home necessary, previously taught, and checked for understanding?

7. Help your child break down an upcoming project/test/assignment/task.

a) Brainstorm every task that needs to be done in order to complete the project.

b) Start with the due date and work backwards to plug in all the tasks. Remember to add in some time to check with the teacher if there are questions.

c) Use an agenda to record what needs to be completed by each date.

d) Get started and check off milestones along the way to the completion date.

We are invested in your success, so please remember to connect with us if you run into any difficulties or need any help with these questions.

You can connect with us at our *Parenting... With A Twist* Facebook page at Facebook.com/parentingwithatwist, or click to parentingwithatwist.com

"The illiterate of the 21st century will not be those who cannot read and write, but those who cannot learn, unlearn and relearn."

- Alvin Toffler

Parenting Tip #9
More Than A Fighting Chance

Why Focus On School

The past chapters have highlighted some of the pitfalls of the traditional education system. We are raising your consciousness of these pitfalls to help you understand that as a parent you will need to supplement your child's education to ensure that they are getting all that they need to enter 'the real world' success-ready. As you've been reading and doing the exercises at the end of each chapter, you will already be putting your child on their path to success. This list will give you the opportunity to be re-engage your child in learning and will also help you to pinpoint some areas you may need to focus on if your work life doesn't inspire you.

Employability Skills Gap

Educational qualifications, job-specific skills, and employability skills are the combined aspects that a person brings to the world of work. Education qualifications are certificates, degrees, and licenses that one requires to work in a certain profession. For example, as a teacher, I needed to get an Education Degree from a recognized university. Job-specific skills consist of the expertise needed to work in a specific field. For example, a web designer would be that they need to understand how to build the back end of a website. Employability skills are necessary for getting, keeping, and doing well on a job. They are needed no matter what field of work you are going into. Therefore, as per our examples, both a teacher and a web designer would need employability skills but they would not need to have each other's educational qualifications or job-related skills.

Employability skills are the foundation of your career building blocks and yet, they are frequently seen as lacking in graduates. This would be why somebody with little to no formal education is able to be wildly successful. According to surveys carried out with employers, these are the skills that will make you more employable: communication, teamwork, problem solving, initiative and enterprise, planning and organizing, self -management, and learning.

Why is there this skills gap between what students are learning in school versus what they need to be successful in the workplace? As I mentioned in an earlier chapter, my son was given the same book that I was given to read for Grade 8 English, twenty-one years ago. At that point in the book I mentioned, how could we look at how phones have changed in twenty-one years but not the curriculum? Along these lines, I'd like to mention another key aspect of the education system that hasn't changed–the classroom. We've had almost the same classroom set-up for one hundred and fifty years. School was originally designed to produce workers that would transition to employment in factories. School wasn't designed for the completely different economy we have now. The Model T was a cutting-edge design for its time, but compare that to the cars we drive today.

To give your child more than a fighting chance and to enable you, as the everyday parent, to understand what is needed to be wildly successful, we have broken down what each of the employability skills mean so that you can ensure your child has access to opportunities to learn these skills.

We don't want you to feel overwhelmed by the fact that as a conscious parent this is your responsibility, so we've also highlighted which chapters you can go to in this book to advance your knowledge to start transforming your child's life today!

1. Mastering The Art of Communication:

Communication skills are ranked first in a job candidate's 'must have' skills and qualities. More than just the words you use, effective communication combines a set of skills including nonverbal communication, engaged listening, managing stress in the moment, communicating assertively, and recognizing and understanding your own emotions and those of the person you're communicating with.

a) Communication & Connection

In writing this section I realized that I was using the word communication a lot. I knew that proper writing style would suggest that I needed to find a synonym for this word so that you wouldn't get tired of seeing the word repeated. The first suggestion of a synonym was connection. I mention this because it's not a word that came to mind; however, upon reflection, it's the perfect word. Communication is all about how well we connect with others and how much others feel connected to us. When you look at communication in this light, you will be able to see why employers look at it as one of the top skills they are looking for. As well, this sense of thinking of communication like connection also explains why communication is a key skill needed for the following sub-topics: interviews, networking, information meetings, how to sell/market yourself, and how you represent yourself. This very important topic is covered extensively in the chapters titled: – "My Mind On My Money, My Money On My Mind," "Grades Do Not Define Intelligence," "The Language of Leadership," "I'm Not A Child Psychologist, I'm 'Just' A Parent."

b) Staying Cool In The Hot Seat

What is a piece of the hiring process? An interview! Interviews provide information about people's communication skills, motivations, feelings, attitudes, and appearance. For example, an interview helps demonstrate a candidate's personality and how They present themselves. They also work to the candidate's benefit by conveying information on workplace culture and how people in an organization treat one another.

Furthermore, there are going to be times in the workplace and at home where you need to remain calm in your delivery of a message whether you are the one delivering the message or receiving it. Managing your emotions enables one to stay cool in the hot seat!

c) Put Your Best Foot Forward

Most competitive companies, such as Google, hire less than 1% of their online external job applicants and 55% of all their jobs are filled through a combination of internal promotions and networking. So, it's not about what you know…it's who you know. And further to that, it's not only who you know, but who knows you! Networking, both in person and on social media, is an important part of planning for your future. The relationships you make now could last for years to come and be of tremendous benefit. To have perfected the art of communication will ensure you are on your way to becoming an outstanding networker.

d) It's Not Just What You Know, It's Who You Know

Another way to actively meet key people in your job industry, as opposed to passively waiting for a job ad, is to conduct information meetings. An informational meeting is an in-person approach to researching a potential career, industry, and corporate culture of a potential future workplace or school. These interviews are meant for gathering information and expanding professional networks.

e) How To Market & Sell Yourself

In order to secure a job once we've networked, conducted information meetings, and been invited for an interview, is to have the ability to sell yourself. Many of us grew up with the conditioning that it's obnoxious to brag or call attention to our achievements. As a result, most people aren't used to talking about themselves, let alone 'selling' themselves. In daily life, we are rarely called upon to list our strengths or detail our accomplishments. This would also be rooted in a firm sense of self-confidence so I invite you to reference the chapters not only on communication but also the ones cited below on confidence.

f) "Who You Are Speaks So Loudly, I Can't Hear What You Are Saying."

Employers make assumptions based on a job candidate's appearance. When I taught career education, I would put a picture of a clown on an overhead with the following saying: "Who You Are Speaks So Loudly, I Can't Hear What You Are Saying." People judge us based on our outward appearance. If we want an opportunity to be taken seriously and our words given merit, we have to be aware of our outward appearance. Children need to be taught how to assess what the corporate culture of their desired work place and how to dress for that culture.

Beyond dress, the ability to adapt and fit in is a key to our very survival, be it in class, at a friend's house, or in the workplace. It's no secret that teachers, parents, and employers look not only at your skills, but how you will fit into their culture. The thought is that you can always be taught that 1 + 1 = 2, but where are you taught things like how to take turns during conversations, maintain eye contact, be polite, repair misunderstandings, find topics of mutual interest, and recognize social cues (both verbal and nonverbal.)

2. Teamwork

Gainful employment is largely based on how well you interact as part of a team as it's difficult to employ someone who doesn't have solid interpersonal skills. Someone who views themselves as part of the team and willing to work within the culture of the workplace is a necessity. Therefore, you need to understand how to build healthy relationships with others. Not only does having the skill of building a healthy relationship help your employment situation but healthy relationships also build self-esteem, improve mental and emotional health, and help you live a fuller, richer life. Conversely, the health risks from being alone or isolated in one's life are comparable to the risks associated with cigarette smoking, high blood pressure, and obesity. More on this topic can be found in the chapters titled: "Money On My Mind, Mind On My Money," "How To Read A Report Card, No Matter What The Grade," "The Language Of Leadership," and "I'm Not A Psychologist, I'm 'Just' A Parent."

3. Problem Solving

We face a universe of rapidly evolving technology, an ever-shifting global economy, and far-reaching health and environmental challenges—scenarios that will require plenty of creative and critical thinkers. Creative and critical thinking are ways of looking at problems or situations from a perspective that is unorthodox. The ability to think, reason, and make sound decisions is crucial for employees desiring to do well and advance.

At home, children can get into trouble for creative thinking and aren't encouraged to continue acting in those ways. For example, when a toddler figures out that they can climb out of their playpen by stacking toys up in a strategic way, they have engaged in creative problem solving. When the parent discovers this, it's treated as if the child did something wrong (like escape from where she was placed) as opposed to something that could be celebrated. In our 'Twisted' way, we even like to suggest that lying is a form of creative problem solving.

Later, at school, creative problem solving and critical thinking aren't encouraged either, as there is typically a right and wrong answer for the questions the teacher assigns. Remember the analogy of a dolphin being made to climb a tree? Our children are made to do things daily at school that don't engage their creative or critical thinking abilities. More on this topic can be found in the chapter titled: "I'm Not A Psychologist, I'm "Just" A Parent."

4. Initiative & Enterprise

Having initiative means being able to work unsupervised and using common sense to anticipate what's needed to solve a problem; to make things happen. It is about not having to ask for help continuously, but also knowing your limits as well as coming up with fresh ideas to help the employer. Enterprising people are good at thinking 'outside the box' to identify efficiencies and to devise ways to find new business opportunities to make more money for the company. This important topic is covered extensively in the chapters titled: "How To Read A Report Card, No Matter What The Grade," "The Dog Ate My Homework And My Study Notes," "The Language of Leadership," "I'm Not A Child Psychologist, I'm "Just" A Parent."

a) Learn to Fail, Fail To Learn

Failure is only a word that human beings use to judge a given situation. Instead of fearing failure, we need to realize that failures, miss takes, and errors are the way we learn and the way we grow. Many of the world's greatest successes have learned how to fail their way to success. At Parenting…With A Twist, we believe in failing early and failing often.

> *Many of the world's greatest successes have learned how to fail their way to success.*

b) How To Love Yourself: Diamond in the Rough

In our initial interviews with families, we ask them to pretend that they are all finished working with us and to describe to us what would be different within their home, for us to know that we were successful. Every single family that we've worked with answer the same way: they want their child's confidence restored. This need transcends, gender, ethnicity, and ability level of the learner, as well as the income level of the family. When a person is confident, they are showing that they have faith in their talents, abilities, and personal strengths. Having confidence has a positive impact on your day-to-day life, as well as your ability to achieve the things you want to do.

c) Entrepreneurship: Don't Boss Me Around

An entrepreneur is someone who sees an opportunity or a gap in what's currently offered in the market place and creates an organization. An entrepreneur is someone who looks at thinks differently; challenges the status quo; knows he or she can do it better or differently. Being an entrepreneur involves quite a lot of initiative and enterprise! Your child can start off small and simple, like a lemonade stand, then dog-walking or lawn-cutting or car-washing or child-minding, etc.

5. Planning and Organizing

There are 1,440 minutes in a day, 7 days in a week and 52 weeks in a year and nothing can change this. Spending your time in a frenzy of activity often achieves less, because you're dividing your attention between so many different tasks. Good time management lets you work smarter–not harder–so you get more done in less time. When you are able to organize and plan how long you will spend on specific activities every day, you will experience less stress and greater opportunities to achieve important life and career goals. This is why we've put such an emphasis on using an agenda and scheduling throughout this book. This is covered more extensively in the chapters titled: "The Dog Ate My Homework And My Study Notes," and "I'm Not A Child Psychologist, I'm "Just" A Parent."

6. Self-Management

Success in life is linked to how well you manage yourself and your life situations, as well as, go to work every day. To be a self-manager, you need to have the ability to regulate your mental health, create successful habits, and have good money management skills. More on this topic can be found in chapters titled: "Mind On My Money, Money On My Mind," "You Are Already Wealthy," "How To Read A Report Card, No Matter What The Grade," "The Language of Leadership," "I'm Not A Psychologist, I'm 'Just' A Parent."

a) Peace of Mind: What Do I Want To Be When I Grow Up?

Instead of feeling from your kids the thought of, "What do I want to be when I GIVE up?" From the time we are in elementary school, people ask us what we want to be when we grow up. This should not be the question, instead, we should ask kids to start asking themselves from an early age: "What do I love to do?" "What is important and means something to me?" "What makes me feel happy?" "What do I care about regardless of any rewards?"

b) How to Create A Habit: Practice Makes Perfect

Habits account for about 40% of our behaviours on any given day. Understanding how to build new positive habits or change one that isn't serving you, is essential for making progress in your health, your happiness, and your life in general. The habits of highly successful people allow them to consistently perform behaviours that breed success. Everything from eating well to responsible spending to task completion and beyond requires habits that make such behaviours part of our daily life. Highly successful people have learned to develop good habits, and it takes discipline, courage and hard work on a daily basis to keep those habits in place.

c) Mental Health: Perfectly Imperfect And Happy…Just Because

Mental health means striking a balance in all aspects of your life: social, physical, spiritual, emotional, economic, and mental. Reaching a balance is a learning process. At times, you may tip the balance too much in one direction and have to find your footing again. Your personal balance will be unique, and your challenge will be to stay mentally and emotionally healthy by keeping that balance. As well, you will want to be able to 'Be Happy…Just Because' no matter what life brings. You aren't waiting for something to happen to make you happy or having your happiness taken away just because something doesn't go your way.

d) Healthy Living: Learn And Burn

Your food choices each day affect your health—how you feel today, tomorrow, and in the future. Good nutrition is an important part of leading a healthy lifestyle. Combined with physical activity, your diet can help you reach and maintain a healthy weight, reduce your risk of serious chronic diseases and promote your overall health. This can help children with improved health, better scholastic achievement, better fitness, feeling happier, maintaining a healthy weight, improving self-confidence, and learning new skills.

e) Financial Literacy Skills

Money is necessary to live and live well in our society, but you don't need a lot of money to be happy, independent, and successful. What you do need is education about money so that you have an understanding of good debt versus bad debt; know your numbers; have savings, investments, giving back and spending money; understand your habits and mindsets around money; have the knowledge of how to use the financial tools available; and how to make sacrifices for longer-term financial goals. This education enables you to take control of your money and make it work for you. Find more information on this topic in the chapters titled: "The Predicators of Success," "My Mind On My Money, My Money On My Mind," "You Are Already Wealthy," and "Setting Up Your Household for Success."

7. Learning

Learning is about wanting to understand new things and being able to pick them up quickly. It's also about being able to take on new tasks and to adapt when the way things are done in the workplace change. This is covered in chapters titled: "Setting Up Your Household for Success," "Please Do Label My Child," "The Dog Ate My Homework And My Study Notes," and "Grades Do Not Define Intelligence."

a) Understanding Your Learning Style: Should A Leopard Change It's Spots?

By recognizing that your child has a unique learning style, the realization that the current one-size-fits-all way of teaching used in our traditional school system is not that effective and should not be the norm. False expectations that every child studies and learns the same way can be replaced with a more realistic outlook. This will make every student's learning experience more positive and enjoyable.

b) Learning Something New: You Can Teach This Dog New Tricks

Learning something new engages your brain in new ways. This can be learning a foreign language, a new computer program, playing an instrument, taking up a new sport… the list is endless! There is a myth that children (and, for that matter, adults) don't really enjoy learning new things, but as every video game maker has realized, the truth is just the opposite, as practically every video game is in part about mastering new skills. Why not start learning something new today? Your brain will thank you for it!

c) Speed Reading: Need for Specd

What if your child could read through their notes, textbooks and work manuals twice as fast as before? Speed reading provides you with the tools and information you need to improve not only the speed that you read, but your comprehension and concentration as well. Reading engages the eyes, ears, mouth, and brain. Speed reading engages these senses even more than normal reading because you use your senses and brain power even more efficiently.

Parenting Skills Questions

Amber Highlighted Stop Sign: Use Caution When Proceeding

How do you role model this? Role modelling is a way of signalling what's appropriate in terms of how you behave, what you do, the activities you engage in, and what you believe. Remember to share these answers with your Accountability Partner!

Circles: Different Lenses We Put On

1. a) Give three examples in your life where having excellent communication skills enables you to have stronger connections with people.

b) Give three examples in your life where having poor communication skills has the potential to do harm to your relationships with people.

c) Share these answers with your child.

Target: S.M.A.R.T. Goal Setting System

2. a) Rate yourself on the employability skills below, on a scale of zero to ten. A score of zero means that you have no skill in that area. A score of ten means that you have mastered that skill.

i. Communication
ii. Staying Cool In The Hot Seat
iii. Put Your Best Foot Forward
iv. It's Not Just What You Know, It's Who You Know
v. Market/Sell Yourself
vi. "Who You Are Speaks So Loudly, I Can't Hear What You Are Saying".
vii. Teamwork
viii. Problem Solving
ix. Initiative and Enterprise
x. Learn to Fail, Fail To Learn
xi. How To Love Yourself
xii. Entrepreneurship: Don't Boss Me Around
xiii. Planning and Organizing
xiv. Self Management
xv. Peace of Mind
xvi. How To Create A Habit
xvii. Mental Health
xviii. Healthy Living
xix. Financial Literacy Skills
xx. Learning
xxi. Understanding Your Learning Style
xxii. Learning Something New
xxiii. Speed Reading: Need for Speed

b) Choose your three lowest rated Employability Skills and make a S.M.A.R.T. plan to work on improving this.

c) Share this plan with your child and with us.

3. a) Do you depend on school to teach your child Employability Skills?

b) Where is your child taught these skills?

c) Identify ways that you can teach your child these skills.

d) It takes a village to raise a child. Identify members of your family, friends and those in your community that could teach your child these skills.

We are invested in your success, so please remember to connect with us if you run into any difficulties or need any help with these questions.

**You can connect with us at our *Parenting…With A Twist*
Facebook page at Facebook.com/parentingwithatwist,
or click to parentingwithatwist.com**

"The problem with communication is the illusion that it's been accomplished."

\- George Bernard Shaw

Parenting Tip #10
The Language Of Leadership

When my children's father and I separated, the kids and I went for group counselling. The children would go in one room to their session and the adults in another room. In our adult group, the leaders shared statistics on how little time parents actually spend communicating with their kids. Studies suggest that parents spend between 3.5 and 19 minutes a day having meaningful conversation with their child. The leaders told us that they were going to share the statistics in the children's group too and that caused me to giggle. My group leader seemed unimpressed when she told me that she didn't find these statistics funny. I shared that with how much I talked through everything with my children, they probably wished that was a realistic statistic for their life!

More Scary Statistics

We are only spending 3.5 to 19 minutes having meaningful conversation with our kids per day. In comparison, teens are spending 540 minutes per day on media. Makes you pause, doesn't it? The good news is all you have to aim for is 20 minutes a day, and you will be exceeding the statistics! Let's look at how to be better communicators with our kids.

Volume of Your Voice

Would you like your children to hear the volume of your voice or hear your words? Often, to get somebody to hear us, we think we need to increase the volume of our voice. When I was teaching 126 special needs students in a day, there were times I just wanted to yell. But, do you know what I learned was more effective? Whispering. I would talk so low that to hear me, the background noise had to stop. They were engaged in what I was saying because I was engaged in what I was saying. Raise the quality of your words, not your voice.

Children As Mirrors

Remember, your children mirror you, even in your communication! The swear word Jesse is saying at daycare. Chances are he picked it up at home. Your little girl with her hands on her hips telling her younger sister to "HURRY UP!" Chances are she's modelling that from someone at home.

If you truly don't recognize it in yourself, then begin to pay attention to who your child's biggest influencers are. Children's mimicking behaviours are a big clue. When my son was in preschool, and it was cleanup time at home, he was quite specific as to how things needed to be done and would even take what I'd cleaned up and move it. I let him clean up on his own at home, even though it might have not been how I would do it, so he would learn the habit. So, I knew he wasn't getting that approach from me and wasn't sure who he was getting it from. I mentioned his behaviours around cleanup time at home to his preschool teacher who proceeded to get red in the face. She told me that she did that. While she was aware that children would bring their parents' expressions and behaviours to school, she never thought of the children bringing her behaviours home! If your profession involves working with children, chances are the child's family has seen some of you in them.

I was at my son's Track & Field meet and there was this sweet, little, three-year-old boy there who had oodles of energy! His parent was watching the older son in his events, and left the toddler with a grandparent in the stands. He and Grandpa were playing a game. The little boy would climb onto the stands beside Grandpa, who would say, "No, no, no!" in a stern voice. Then, the little boy would jump off the stand. If Grandpa forgot to say, "No, no, no!" the little boy would look at him and say, "Say no." then jump. The little boy was giggling and the Grandpa was laughing too. Cute game, eh?

Later, the father came back to the stands and said "No" to the boy when he wanted to have Dad's phone. The boy grabbed it, threw it, and said, giggling: "You said no!" The father looked as though he was ready to discipline his child. I explained to him the game that the Grandpa and the boy had just been playing. (Try explaining to a three year old the difference between a real "No" and a joking "No.") It's important to get curious with your child as to where their behaviour is coming from.

Keep the above story in mind with whomever the child is spending time with. If it's with grandparents, a co-parent or a daycare worker, then be aware they may have different methods of communication than you do. Clarify differences and effects with your child and with the other influencers. Get creative as to how you might explain the differences. For example, with the story above: "Grandpa has one set of rules and we have another. It's not that either is right or wrong but it's just the way it is." Think of how you will be setting them up for success by teaching them that people have different expectations and communication styles early in life! From parents to teachers to coworkers to bosses to coaches…everyone has different styles of communication.

> *It's important to get curious with your child as to where their behaviour is coming from.*

Keep the Lines of Communication Open

As children get older and you are seeing behaviours or expressions in them that you'd prefer not to see, it's a good idea to get to know who their key influencers are. Always keep your child and their friends close. Be the house they want to hang out at, even if it means your grocery bill goes up. Why? Because you will get to stay in touch with who your child is and what makes them tick. You will get to see what's shaping who they are going to be, beyond your influence. And you will establish communication and trust with their friends too.

This highlights another factor in communicating for success: keep the lines of communication open with everybody in your child's life. If you know your child responds well to their coach, instead of thinking of it as a competition, embrace that. Let the coach know that your child thinks highly of them. Also, if there is an issue, like homework not being completed, see if the coach will have a talk with your child. Remember…it takes a village to raise a child.

Be prepared that even when you are the most fantastic parent EVER, especially after reading this book, that your child will still say that Coach Bob said to study hard for their test, so they rush to get home and study. Even though you could have said that seven million times! Use other mentors to your advantage instead of being frustrated by them.

One of the biggest things I knew growing up was that I could tell my parents anything. This meant that I could call at 2am when I was supposed to be home at 12pm, tell them that my ride had been drinking and ask them to come and get me. I knew that I would have a natural consequence to this, but I also knew they loved me more than they would not love the choice I had made. Correct the behaviour, love the person!

Love your child more than the choices they make.

Self-Talk

We know that we are our children's biggest role models, so start monitoring your thoughts and words for negativity. Things like judgement, worrying, complaining, criticizing, and permission to procrastinate. As these thoughts occur, remind yourself that you have the choice to make your world heaven or hell, just by what you think. A moment of compassion for yourself when you consciously change your words can change your entire day. A string of moments can change the course of your life. Be kind to yourself!

Key Influencers

Our children's key influencers have a great deal of power in relation to forming your child's confidence and the way they see the world. You want to be cognizant of who they are, as well as the power they hold. Who else would become influential people in your child's life? Certainly their other parent(s), their teachers, a friend's parent, a family member, a tutor, a coach. As our children grow up, their circle of influence grows.

Some influences we will appreciate, others not so much. Your child will be watching how you interact with both the people you appreciate and the people you don't. Be mindful of this, especially if you are in a conflict with one of your child's key influencers. You want to role model disagreeing with the behaviour while not attacking the person.

Another tactic is suggesting to your child that they have different people's perspectives to look at. So, if they are struggling with one of their key influential people, like a teacher, they can contrast and compare with the others. What was the same as their favourite teacher? What is different from their favourite teacher? You are emphasizing that the traits are just different, and one is not good, nor the other one bad. It's quite amazing where you can use this communication strategy. You can use it when talking about a co-parent's parenting style, a coach's coaching style, and/or the way a friend's family structures their media time. The most important thing to point out to your child is that as they move forward in life, they get to choose which pieces, from all their different influencers, they want to incorporate into their own lives.

Children are also starting to formulate the type of person they want to be. If they see a trait they aren't happy with in a friend, they can start to articulate what it is about that trait that is uncomfortable for them. You can help them realize that it's just different from how they choose to be. Armed with this knowledge, they can decide to accept the behaviour because they love the person. Or, they can choose to have a conversation with their friend about the behaviour, knowing that they can't accept it, but still want that person in their lives. This is why you keep the dialogue open with your children. You want to help shape them, right? These moments are the ones that will guide your child in a positive direction on their life's journey.

And, besides, what is 'normal'? Isn't it just a setting on a dryer?

Parent First, Friend Second, Principal Third

Parents need to understand that they are their child's parent first and their friend second. Sometimes it's easier to be their friend because you don't have to maintain consistent, firm boundaries or realize that as they continue to grow, you are the main person responsible for them.

A funny story to shed some light on this! When my eldest son was five, one day he was in full-day kindergarten and the next day was in full-day preschool. I picked him up from preschool one afternoon and I was told that he didn't listen to anything. He didn't eat when it was snack time or lie down when it was nap time, colour when it was colouring time, go outside when it was outside time and well...you get the picture. He did whatever he wanted. Being that I was a teacher and he was my child, how do you think I felt? This was unusual behaviour for him as he was the kind of child who usually asks, "How high?" when you say, "Jump!" So, I was curious to have a conversation about what prompted his decision to act that way.

He didn't want to talk about his behaviour on the drive home so I waited until after he'd had a snack. Then, while we were walking our dog, I asked him what happened to cause him to act that way. He told me that there was no principal at preschool, so what were they going to do if he didn't follow the rules?

I'm thinking...OMG...he's gotten in trouble at kindergarten and that's how he knows about the principal. But, how did I not know that he'd gotten into trouble? Why didn't the school call me? Instead of jumping to any conclusions (other than in my head!) I asked him how he knew that. Remember, you can make your head a heaven or hell depending on the stories you create.

This is how he connected the dots: he was at kindergarten in assembly where they introduced the role of the principal. In his mind, the message he heard was that the buck stopped with the principal. If you misbehaved, you went straight to the principal in their office. When he went to preschool the next day he asked where the principal was and where the principal's office was. They told him there wasn't a principal or a principal's office. So, he decided he didn't need to follow the rules as there wasn't anybody to enforce them!

Now, secretly, I was smiling because, how smart is that? However, outwardly, I suggested that I was the principal of any situation he found himself to be in. And, that when you are sent to deal with me, as the principal, there will be consequences. As a parent, our child's behaviour is a reflection of us, but it's also our responsibility. So, he had a choice to change his behaviour at preschool, with seeing me as the principal. For those of you that are wondering…he changed his behaviour.

We also had a conversation about the role of a princiPAL. I could help him work through situations in which he didn't know the right choice or had already made the wrong one; the princiPAL was there to help too. That also lead us into identifying other people in his life that were his key influencers and what different roles and titles they had. For instance, in our tutoring agency, I refer to us as coaches or cheerleaders. So we are Math Coaches and Reading Cheerleaders! Helping your child identify who the cheerleaders and coaches are in their world will provide them with a healthy place to go when they need support. Their confidence will rise when they can point out their cheerleaders—people who believe they can do it, support them in getting there, and lift them back up when they fall.

When my son was older, I shared this story with him and told him that I loved that he was able to use his creative problem solving skills to figure out how to do what he wanted. I told him that this skill set would serve him well later in life. While not wanting to crush his creativity, at five years of age, he couldn't have been safely making choices for how to care for himself all day.

Listen to Hear, Not to Talk

Being a teacher, an avid researcher and a passionate reader, I thought my children should have come out of my womb knowing how to read! My son's Grade 3 teacher called me in to suggest that there were comprehension issues with him. She thought that there was something "wrong" with him and wanted him to undergo some special testing to define specifically what was "wrong."

I had to admit to her that it was simply because he wasn't reading. Yes, I said "admit." This was partly in jest but also partially serious. How could a teacher's son not be reading? I was embarrassed. I share this with you so that you realize that this was my reaction to my own embarrassment which was to do with my thoughts of the way it 'should' be instead of the way it was.

How could my son understand the questions asked when he wasn't reading the material? I emphasized to the teacher that I had done everything on 'the learn-to-read checklist' to ensure he would be an early and voracious reader.

When my son and I sat down to talk about this non-reading issue and how it was starting to affect his schooling, he was able to tell me that comics were where it was at for him. They engaged him. And guess what? He started coming to the library with me enthusiastically to get more comics, and whizzing through comprehension questions at school.

My son taught me something that wasn't on 'the learn-to-read checklist'—what we, as parents, teachers, coaches, etc. might perceive as 'normal' or 'right' isn't always the case. When I didn't see what he wanted to read as the 'right' reading materials, I shut him down. When I heard his words and supported him, he blossomed. What you feed, grows, right? I had to change the books he was 'allowed' to read, not change him. We found the right books to feed him!

In the words of Maya Angelou: "I've learned that people will forget what you said, people will forget what you did, but people will never forget how you made them feel." As this experience happened when my son was in Grade 3, he may not remember what the conversation was about; but he'd remember the feeling of what it was like to talk to me, the next time he had something important to share.

As he grew up, reading comics turned into a love of graphic novels. Graphic novels are a book-length comic that can be fiction, non-fiction, and anthologized works. Considering libraries have whole sections of graphic novels, that tells you how valued and popular they are. Now, the son who wasn't reading in Grade 3 told me in Grade 10 that he wants to work …where? At a library!

Thank Your Children For The Lessons They Teach You

I thanked my son for giving me this new outlook, as with him being my eldest, this valuable lesson ensured I could be a better Mom to the rest of my children–both my biological children, my bonus children, and all the children I've helped in the course of my career. As a result of this experience with my eldest, I encourage any and all reading materials now from cereal boxes to comics to magazines to books; not just books. One step further, I explored why comics and graphic novels appealed to him and I learned something pretty cool. As an auditory learner, he loves the way comics and graphic novels are written as often they are written like a conversation. Auditory learners like to have conversations on topics as opposed to reading about them. In linking that knowledge to how comics and graphic novels are written was a valuable lesson for me as an educator. Since this discovery, we've helped countless families engage their children in reading.

Have the conversations with the key people in your child's life and be open to the fact that 'normal' truly is only the setting on a dryer. Don't define your life or your child's on what the norm is thought to be!

Get Curious

I also want to share that I approached my son's reading not punitively, but with curiosity and empathy. I invite you to do the same: get curious with your children and empathetic to where they are at in their lives. Ask questions! Find out what makes them tick! Find out their 'why'!

I could have reacted negatively to my embarrassment that a teacher said there was something wrong with my child and had to confess it was because he didn't read. You will have many opportunities to change a mood and select your words, but there isn't an opportunity to replace your words once they've escaped. So choose wisely!

Don't Embarrass Your Child

With all my years of teaching and parenting, I would like to drive home the point of not embarrassing your child. I see time after time, parents embarrassing their children in front of others, coaches in front of the team, and teachers embarrassing their students in front of the class. It doesn't resolve anything and it creates a hurt that won't allow a child to open up to you. I believe people do this if they are embarrassed about the situation; thinking it reflects badly on them. They simply don't know how to deal with it or they are using their position of power. As we have learned, language is harmful and it's hard to erase words once they've been said. On the flip side, we've also learned that we can teach kids to be resilient (through the 'elastic band trick' which is later in this chapter) by not allowing others to affect them or change their view of themself.

I also shared my son's reading story to illustrate that you need to be in sync with your child so that you aren't defining them or letting the system define them. What if I didn't know my son couldn't read and I took the teacher's words to heart? What if I then started to treat my child as though there was something wrong with him? What if he was then labelled in that way? I could have had a fixed mindset on his abilities which could have defined him as a non-reader at the age of seven. In our work at Parenting…With A Twist, we often see that outcome with a child who has been defined as not able to do math or read. If you start turning a child off at age seven from the fundamentals of education— literacy and numeracy—how do you expect them to continue to engage? Remember, it takes six positive comments to undue one negative one.

Perhaps your child just isn't that chatty, so how could you these talks with them? Meet them where they are at. My youngest son was having a hard time going to school. Again, another school-related issue that a teacher's child was having. Remember that teachers are humans too and their kids could be experiencing the same things as yours, or in their career they've come across a child that has experienced that. I couldn't always get my son to share how he was feeling as maybe sometimes he didn't know himself. What I did know was that he loved Lego! So I found a Lego-head feeling chart. Contact us if you would like us to send you a jpeg of one. (Our contact information can be found at the end of each chapter in the "Parenting Skills Question" section.) He could point to a couple of heads that he related to. This began a dialogue about feelings and emotions which would sometimes lead to more dialogue and sometimes not. The important piece is that he knew he could engage no matter how he was feeling and that it would be discussed with love and curiosity, not with punishments and discipline.

> *It takes six positive comments to undue one negative one.*

Blind Trust

There doesn't have to be blind trust in your child's teacher or any another key influencer as they are not the expert on your child. Get curious when talking to them! Ask why they are suggesting what they are suggesting. Ask for their proof of what they are saying to be true. Ask for other possible factors that could be contributing. And ask for other members of their team to be present when somebody suggests, "There is something wrong with your child." Choose one of your child's 'cheerleaders.' Remember I asked the principal to be apart of a teacher-parent meeting about my son's report card, not only as the manager of the teacher but as a cheerleader for my son. In getting curious, you can start to see if there are any patterns in your child's behaviours. For example: if the behaviour happens in one environment and not another, what is the root cause of the behaviour? What can we change to make the environment a safe place for your child?

> *In getting curious, you can start to see if there are*
> *any patterns in your child's behaviours.*

Since school is where children spend most of their childhood, I urge you to engage with the school. I would suggest you introduce yourself to your child's teacher prior to teacher-parent conferences. Check in with them about what would work best to keep in regular contact: email, agenda, phone call. If you only start engaging when your child is in trouble, then you haven't developed a rapport to begin to build bridges. Plan to volunteer at school! There are many opportunities with various time commitments. Research shows that students thrive, whose parents volunteer at school. In the "Parenting Skills Questions" section of the book in earlier chapters, we have laid out the steps to forming solid relationships with your child's teacher.

Your Child Needs Their Voice

Some of you might be thinking that it would be pretty awesome to have a child that was like a robot and did what they were told, exactly when they were told. Let me tell you from firsthand experience, you don't want this. I was brought up to be 'the nice girl.' This meant that I did what I was told and what was expected of a 'nice girl.' I was as close to a robot as you could imagine!

Guess what happened to me? My voice, metaphorically speaking, was not really developed, never mind heard. I rarely spoke my mind on issues related to me. I held my thoughts in, even though it was slowly killing me inside. I was scared of being perceived as not being 'the nice girl.' I was scared of what people would think of that and I never wanted to upset someone.

Encourage your child to speak up and to not be scared to say what's on their mind. They need to have an outlet and wouldn't you prefer that outlet be you? If they do keep it inside, sooner or later it's going to come out, and it might be in an unhealthy way. Like the child who has a tantrum over some seemingly little thing. When you talk it through, it becomes clear their emotions were triggered by something earlier that they weren't able to talk about. Think about a time when something upsetting happened at work and you got home and took it out on your unsuspecting partner.

We need to encourage our child to hear and feel their own gut feelings. When we have the mentality that kids should just do what they are told to do, we strip them of their ability to have a gut feeling and act on it. Our instincts guide us and let us know what is best for us. My mom went to a talk by the police when I was in Elementary school. The officers at the talk suggested that if people trusted their gut instincts more, fewer crimes would happen. People often share that they had a feeling something bad was going to happen to them before it actually did, and instead of acting on the feeling, they talked themselves out of it. My mom woke me up to tell me she was sorry she hadn't trusted my gut and that she would listen to me in future. Here's why…

I had a friend who always wanted me to go to her house for a play date. I often did but when she had a particular uncle over, I didn't feel comfortable going there. One day, the uncle wanted to take my friend and I out for donuts. My mom said "Yes" for me. As soon as we stopped at the donut place and he got out, I ran all the way home. My mom was quite upset with me and said I needed to apologize. I did, but I refused to go for a visit while that uncle was visiting. That was very unusual behaviour for 'the nice girl!' It turns out the uncle was charged with sexual assault of minors. Please teach your child to listen to their inner voice and to say "No" with confidence.

When we have the mentality that kids should just do what they are told to do, we strip them of their ability to have a gut feeling and act on it, as well we take away their voice and the ability to know how to use it.

Your Child Must Know How To Say "No" & Change Their Mind

Does your child know how to say no or change their mind…with confidence, ease and even some humour thrown in? Our society is set up to teach children to be people pleasers: to always say "Yes" to their parents, teachers, and other people of authority. And we label a child as a trouble maker when they say "No."

Then the child turns into a teen and we want them to "Just say no." when they get into awkward, intense, potentially life-changing situations. Like, "Just say no" to drugs. Or, "Just say no" to sex. Or, "Just say no" to drinking and driving and more currently, texting and driving. In all of these conversations, we emphasize that they understand why they need to say "No." For example, drinking and driving can lead to the wrecked car they show us every year at the "Just Say No Drinking & Driving" assembly. Now they even take kids to the morgue to really drill the point in as to why you shouldn't drink and drive. However, statistics would suggest that people still drink and drive, even adults.

So, kids can recite back to us the 'why' of not doing something, but where do our kids get to practice the just saying no. The times where your child has practiced saying no to you, I'm sure hasn't gone over very well. What about when they've said it to their teacher or coach?

Let Your Child Say "No" To You

I hate to be the one to break it to you, but you are going to have to let your child practice saying no to you. And, sure, you can do scenarios where they practice some prescribed answers. Like when they are offered drugs and they say: "No, I have a game tomorrow." Role paying with your child is great as you can come up with answers to different pressure situations and add humour to their responses. Role playing will also help the answers roll more easily off their tongues as they will have had practice!

Kids will also need some unrehearsed times to be allowed to say "no" so that they can do it with confidence. Although you may not like it, find some things that you are okay with them saying "no" to you about. They need the confidence to spontaneously be able to say "no" if something comes up that they haven't rehearsed. Plus, it would be great to teach them that saying "no" to you is okay. As they develop their own thoughts, ideas and opinions outside of ours, as parents, that sometimes make us want to hold a little tighter to our kids. However, it's a chance for them to find out who they are and about consequences to actions.

For instance, if a child says they don't want to wear gloves, the natural consequence of this is that their hands will be cold. They will decide in the future if that's something they want to do. As they get older, you'll want to allow them some bigger opportunities to say "No."

Saying "Yes" To Something Is Saying "No" To Something Else

"No" can feel like a weighty thing to say as you may feel that you are letting the person down. However, another way to look at this is that when you say "yes" to somebody else you could potentially be saying "no" to yourself. We, as adults, do this a lot when we take on extra responsibilities. Your boss asks you to work extra hours and you have plans. If you say "no" you are afraid he won't ask you again, so you say "yes." By saying "yes" to your boss, you've just told your child, whom you had plans to make a special dinner with, that your work is more important to you. On the flip side, if you said "no" to your boss, explaining that you have important plans that night but would be willing to do it the next night, you are letting your boss know that you are hearing their words and that your time is valuable. In the future, your boss would realize that they need to ask you ahead of time if they want you to stay late. You've just taught your boss how to treat you by how you let them treat you! If you always say "yes", then don't be surprised that your boss always asks you to work late at the last minute and doesn't seem to respect your time.

Teaching your child at an early age that saying "yes" to something means saying "no" to something else, and that how we let people treat us is how they will treat us, is invaluable. Think of the success you are setting them up for: defining your values, teaching people how to treat you, and valuing yourself!

A line I heard recently was: "No, all by itself, is a full sentence." Quite often, we believe if we say "no" we must give an explanation. And yet, when we say "yes" we hardly get it out our mouth before the person is on to the next request! Start observing what happens when you say "no."

In knowing how quickly a "yes" is accepted, we need to make sure our child knows it's okay to change their mind, with confidence, ease, and humour. This allows for a child to take responsibility by re-addressing the situation to make sure their voice is heard. So they take responsibility for having said "yes" and have the right to change their mind. Think of a time you may have over-committed yourself and didn't feel it was okay to change your mind. Let's not have our children fall into that trap.

I was an adult before I realized that I could say "no" with confidence. It was so foreign to me that I had to practice. I went to stores that had high pressure commission sales people and practiced saying "no." Part of me felt bad because I was taking the sales people's valuable time; however, I knew that I needed to practice saying "no" enough that it would feel natural for me to do so.

Other Responses To Ensure Your Child Knows How To Say

The other response we can practice with our children is: "I need some time to think about that." That way, if there is a situation they aren't sure of or find difficult, they don't have to feel obligated to give an answer. Again, remember with all these responses and behaviours, we are instilling that we also have to accept it when our children say it to us!

Another very powerful sentence we can teach our children is: "I've changed my mind." Again, just like above, if they've felt pressured in a situation and given an answer that they would like to change, you've given them the means to do so. Your child feels pressured to have sex with their boyfriend so she agrees to do so. In talking it over with friends, and hopefully you, she decides she isn't ready. Give her the confidence and ease to say that she's changed her mind!

Discipline & Communication

Parents use discipline when they feel their child is behaving inappropriately. We've mentioned in earlier chapters to discipline using natural consequences as much of the time as you can. What you also need to be aware of when you are disciplining your child is how you communicate.

It's important to not ridicule or shame your child so that you keep the child's self-esteem intact. This way of communicating maintains your connection with your child so that they will continue to seek your advice and follow your guidance. As I mentioned previously, I always knew that I could call home. Even when it was past curfew and I suggested I needed a ride home because my ride had been drinking. I want that for you with your children because the consequences of a child not being able to phone home, in ANY situation, could be dire.

You want to create a safe environment for them to talk to you. Sometimes that may not happen in the first conversation about the subject which is why it's so important to keep the doors of communication open. Create this environment by being neutral and not attacking while taking the appropriate disciplinary steps. This does not mean that they will always like or appreciate your direction, but you can know that you will be helping them to grow, mature, and become more responsible in the long term.

Healthy Conflict Is Healthy

A super important part of communication is how to deal with conflict. We illustrated that above with the "just say no" conversation. Conflicts will arise. Many times, it's thought of as unhealthy. All conflict is doing is letting people know they don't see a situation the same way.

If you think about it, how can people see a situation the same way? I was born, raised and observed the world through my eyes as it's unfolded for me. Just as you were born, raised and observed the world through your eyes as it unfolded for you. Remember: we each have our own lifeline which creates the lens through which we see the world.

How we observe the world dictates how we react to the world. If I was shown love through physical touch, growing up, and was told that gifts were a shallow way to show love, then when someone shows me physical affection, I will translate that to mean love. And if somebody bought me a gift, I could think they are shallow. If my partner was shown love through gifts and never received any physical touch, then when someone buys him something, he will translate that to mean love and he most likely won't seek out physical touch. Imagine these two people in a relationship. One is buying the other gifts and he doesn't understand why his partner doesn't understand that he loves her. Meanwhile, the other partner wants to come home every night and cuddle, and thinks that when their partner doesn't want to do that, he doesn't really love her. We have a conflict here, in how two people see and react to the world.

What happens next? Research tells us that we fight, flight or freeze in a challenging situation. Fighting could mean that both partners would insist their way is the right way. Flight could mean that the person who wasn't getting physical touch may go elsewhere to find it. And freeze might be that the partner who doesn't like physical attraction shuts down to any sort of touch. I am giving a partner example instead of a parent-child example as it's important for children to see conflict between adults and, then see it resolved. Think of how successful they will be as a partner if you have taught them that people see the world through different lenses, and how to compromise in those situations. This sets them up for success in their personal, school, and work life!

What is good to discuss with your children is that all of this is normal. It's normal to not see a situation just as someone else has. It's normal to fight, flight or freeze because it's what our bodies are programmed to do. And that once you learn to communicate, especially in conflictual situations, you get to be like a super hero of communication! Just like anything, the more practice with it, the better you become.

Do you know what is essentially happening in a conflict? In the simplest sense, people's opinions, thoughts, and words just want to be heard. And the Communication Process can help us understand how to do that.

The Communication Process

Let's break down the Communication Process into singular terms: Sender, Language, Method, Receiver, Decoding, and Feedback.

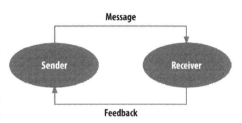

A 'sender' is the party that sends a message in a particular language through a particular means to a target. Different means include speaking, writing, video transmission, audio transmission, electronic transmission through emails, text messages and faxes, and even nonverbal communication, such as body language. The target is the 'receiver' of the message. The receiver must decode the message for understanding and send feedback to the sender so that they know the message was received.

Communication Breakdown

Now let's see where communication can break down:

-What if the sender sends the message in a language the target doesn't understand? How often do you hear a child suggest that they didn't understand what the teacher was saying? Perhaps the teacher was using language specific to the topic within that subject that the student had never heard before.

If the student has the confidence to tell the teacher that they've never heard the terms the teacher is using before and they are lost, the hope would be that the teacher would explain the terms and check for understanding before moving on.

-What if the sender sends the message through printed text to the target but the target's text function isn't working properly? How often do we hear that somebody hasn't responded to a text and all of a sudden there is an assumption that the person is mad at them! Or, how often do we assume a certain 'tone' to a cell phone text or an email?

The sender could decide to phone the target to say they had sent some texts, but there was no response and they are left wondering what was up. By phoning the person, you are eliminating any story as to why the target didn't respond. And, when we add our own interpretation of the 'tone' to an incoming text or email, are we creating a 'story'? When we give our feedback to the sender, we should check in if that is the tone the sender intended. Don't believe everything you think! It's all relative to what story you create about it.

-What if the sender sends a message and it goes to the wrong target? You tell your child to be home right after school as they have a dentist appointment. When you said it, both children were getting out of the car in a rush to get to school on time and the child who had the appointment didn't hear it, and they don't show up right after school.

If your child says they thought you were talking to their sibling about the dentist appointment, you don't even have a conflict because it's not that they intentionally didn't listen to your words. This is a typical case of distraction. With the amount of electronic gadgets today, distractions are quite common.

-What if the receiver gets the message and decodes it wrong? On a Monday, the teacher suggests that the homework is due the next day. On the Tuesday, the class has a field trip. So, the majority of students think the teacher meant the homework was due on the Wednesday and don't complete their work for the Tuesday.

If your child explains to the teacher their interpretation of when the work is due, from how they heard it and wrote it down in their agenda, that takes the fight out of the conflict. Both parties can form a new understanding, moving forward.

Reducing Conflict

What we can see from the above examples is that when we don't provide feedback, we cannot check for understanding. When we don't check for understanding, we have no idea if the message was received how the sender intended it to be. One of the easiest ways to check for understanding, and ultimately, to have less conflict, is to have the receiver repeat the message.

In resolving conflict, it's important for the receiver to ensure they are getting the message clearly. This will determine if there is even anything worth having a conflict over. In some of those examples, the two parties may have to agree to disagree and look for what can be different next time.

In the dentist appointment scenario, some options could be to have the child, whose appointment it was, repeat the request back and/or have them write the appointment on a sticky and put it in their lunch bag or write it in their agenda. Thereby ensuring that the child got the message.

Let's see another way to resolve conflict.

Resolving Conflict Like A Four Year Old

My four-year-old son had gone hiking with a friend, Nicole, and her mom, Michelle. Michelle phoned me after the hike and asked if my son could stay longer as they were making a cake. I said sure and asked if the cake was for anything special. She told me that

Nicole had hit my son and when Nicole apologized, my son had said that sorry was just a word and really didn't mean much to him. When asked what would make him feel better, my son proceeded to say making a cake and singing him Happy Birthday would make him feel great! Could you imagine—we all go into adulthood thinking that if we simply bake somebody a cake, all would be well in the world! Wow, what a world that would be. I dare you to try it next time you've had a disagreement with someone.

Dealing With Different Personality Types

We all have certain personalities that we deal with on a daily basis. There is the complainer who always thinks the worst is always going to happen. We have the clever person who tends to make situations seem more complex than they actually are and likes to be in charge. We have the knowledgeable person who can come across as arrogant and blind to their own limitations. We have the anxious person who has a hard time making a decision because all the 'what ifs' of certain scenarios come into play. We have the person who seems like they are on the edge, and we never know what is going to send them into anger. There is the negative person that complains about everything. Oh! And there is the poor-me person that always has bad things happening to them. And of course, the 'they can't do it without me' person. Then, there is that calm person that you know is able to deal with whatever life throws at them and just be. They seem to be happy…just because!

Your goal as a conscious parent raising success-ready kids is to have them strive to be the calm person who is happy…just because. Why? Life can throw some curve balls and if we are already somebody who tends to see the negative, then the curve balls could send us spiralling out of control.

Start to observe your children. What is their dominant personality? Are you able to see circumstances and situations where they fluctuate between different personality types? Why is it easier to be happy…just because, in some situations and negative, anxious or angry in other situations?

Triggers

When you start observing, you will be able to identify different triggers which seem to bring out the worst or the best in your child. I'll give you a personal example. I allow my children's father to trigger me. Pay particular attention to the fact that I said, "I allow." It is not up to my children's father to not trigger me, it's up to me.

In an ideal world, he and I would sit down, go over the things that trigger both of us and do our best to avoid doing those things to each other. But let's get real, if we weren't able to do this and save our relationship when we lived together, it's a stretch to think that we'd be able to do this after the fact. However, I have to interact with him and when I allow myself to get triggered, I turn into somebody I don't quite like. I observed this about myself and made a conscious effort to change it.

My youngest son's biggest trigger is when he perceives that the other children in the house are treating him in a certain way because he's the youngest. Important to note that I said "perceives." He doesn't actually know for a fact that when his siblings are saying whatever they are saying, it's because he's the youngest. But that's the story he's made up in his head and that story triggers him. This is important for him to know because only he can change the story. It's also important for the family to know so we can choose to not highlight the fact that he's the youngest. This is an example of where people can sit down and work through their triggers together. It's still up to him to change the story, but we can all support him on his journey.

Our other son was triggered when we would join hands and sing "Kumbaya." Yes, we used to do that! One day, my children were fighting in the car and I didn't want to yell at them to stop yelling, so instead, I said that if they didn't stop they could join hands and sing "Kumbaya." It became our family 'go-to.' Whenever one of us was having a rather large melt down, we knew "Kumbaya" was not far behind. And yes, if you saw a family doing that in the airport on their way to Disneyland and again multiple times at Disneyland, that was us. Although Disneyland is said to be "The Happiest Place On Earth," I beg you to realize that hot sun, hungry kids, big line ups, late nights, junky food, multiple personalities (not mine, the ten people we were there with) and the constant adrenaline highs, sometimes make for some not so happy times on Earth.

My son doesn't enjoy physical touch—at all! As well, the song "Kumbaya" rubbed him the wrong way. So having to join hands and sing it had the opposite effect on him that we wanted. Instead, we changed it to Bob Marley's song, "Three Little Birds" where "...every little thing gonna be alright..." He could sing along with us and be part of our calming exercise and he didn't need to hold hands with us to have the same effect.

The first step is key: find out what your child's triggers are. When you don't know what you don't know, it's kind of hard to do anything about it! Next, determine if it's a story that they've made up. Then get curious! Can the trigger be taken care of by a simple conversation with someone? Can they make a compromise to alleviate the trigger?

> ***When you don't know what you don't know, it's kind of hard to do anything about it!***

We've worked with many individuals over the years that realize that they have triggers and don't know what to do about them. We've given some examples above to help. While it's up to the individual to control their reactions, as we cannot control other people, we can still discuss our triggers in order to find other solutions.

Happy…Just Because

How do we get our child to the point of being happy…just because, no matter what is happening around them and who they are dealing with? By teaching them to realize that they only have control over their own reactions. They cannot control the other person's negativity or anxiousness, but they can control their reaction to it.

Throughout our life, we deal with people who are going to rub us the wrong way. The key is to treat what they are saying as if it's exactly what you want to hear. When you are asking your child to get ready for bed and they give you some attitude about it, take their tone, language, volume, etc. out of it and pretend they are saying: "Of course I'll go get ready for bed." Then, continue the conversation with them. When you don't fuel the fire, it has nowhere to go but out!

Raise the quality of your words, not the volume of your voice.

I use this strategy with my youngest son who can get fiery quite quickly. It works almost every time. I've been doing this with him for a while, simply because I didn't know how else to deal with his anger. Anger is so opposite to my being that I had to learn to remove the emotion and speak to him as though he'd just said exactly what I wanted to hear. What's great about this too is that I'm role modelling for him what to do when he gets angry in the future or somebody raises their voice to him.

When using the above strategy doesn't work, I use humour. Just as you wouldn't fight fire with fire, you'd use water; it's the same principle. My humour is genuine; it's not sarcasm because I want to calm the fire, not inflame it.

Another way to deflect another's emotional state is to simply say the way the person is feeling back to them, not taking responsibility for their feelings, but in acknowledgement of them. You are not responsible for another's feelings but to acknowledge them is a loving act of compassion!

When your child is really ready to make the change themselves, how can you help them? Here is the good old elastic band trick!

The Elastic Band Trick

Have the conversation with your child about what they would like to see shift. Suggest to them that you are going to explain an exercise to them that will help them make this shift. Make sure you have this conversation before actually doing the exercise! Get an elastic band. Put it on their wrist. Have them make the conscious choice that they are not going to allow their identified triggers to change their mood. When a situation happens and their mood is changed in an undesirable way, your child needs to take the elastic band off and put it on their other wrist. Anytime they allow their mood to be changed negatively, they take the band off and put it on the other wrist. Psychology suggests that it takes anywhere from twenty-two to ninety days to change a habit. So your child will be cured of this trigger if after twenty-two to ninety days they have not moved the elastic. And, you've also helped your child rewire their brain!

Imagine the power your child now holds. Bully at school, mean kid on the playground, negative co-worker—Boom! They've learned to master their moods and their communications.

While you are doing this rewiring, treat your child with oodles of love and care. It's huge for someone to realize that there is something they want to shift in their life. It's a whole other level of awesomeness when they actual start that act of shifting it. Remember when they were learning to walk or ride their bike? Have the same expectations with this process. Know that they will fall and be there for all the miss takes it takes to get them to where they want to be. Then, celebrate this accomplishment with them!

Our Language

The age-old saying "stick and stones may break my bones, but words will never hurt me" implies that words are not damaging. They are. Use them with care. Teach your child to use them with care.

In our house, one of the four-letter words we don't use is: can't. I instill in my children, and in those I work with, the belief that you can do anything you put your mind, body, and soul into. And the flip side of that is that you can also choose not to do something. So instead of saying, "I can't do that," I ask my children and those I work with to say, "I'm choosing not to do that." That leaves the power with them if they decide to do it in the future as they've not limited themselves by saying can't. Watch where you or your children say can't. And even more important, where somebody has said can't to you or you have said it to your child. As mentioned in the money chapter, when we say "We can't afford that," we are cutting off any solutions to how the item or service could be afforded.

Other self-limiting words that I bring people's attention to are: never, should and always. It's very easy to put something off if you think you are never going to be able to do it. "I'm never going to be able to do this math question." So the mind automatically goes to, why even try it then? Where do you limit yourself by thinking you will never do something or suggest that to your child about their abilities?

As soon as we say should, we are not fully invested in the action. "I really should call this person back." "I really should do the laundry." I equate having the shoulds to having the shits. You don't really want to have the shits as that means you've lost control of your bowels! We can either embrace it or resist it. What happens when you resist having it? Think of using the word, should, like that. You are either going to embrace calling the person back or don't do it. You decide whether you are going to have a life where you are constantly doing your shoulds (having the shits) or you are going to be in control of what you want to do (not having the shits). You take your power back!

Always is a lot like never, just on the flip-side! "She is always late." "My boss always says no." Well guess what? With using that language, more often than not, she will be late and your boss will say no! Because you've expected those responses, you won't engage any further than that.

Self-limiting words lead to self-limiting thoughts, actions, habits etc. This quote sums it up quite nicely:

> *Watch your thoughts, for they become words.*
>
> *Watch your words, for they become actions.*
>
> *Watch your actions, for they become habits.*
>
> *Watch your habits, for they become character.*
>
> *Watch your character, for it becomes your destiny.*
>
> *(Lao Tzu)*

Balancing Limiting Thoughts

Try changing your child's limiting thought to a positive thought:

Limiting Thought:	Change The Thought To:
I'm not good at this.	What am I missing to help me get better?
I give up.	I'll use the strategies I've learned and keep trying!

Limiting Thought:	Change The Thought To:
This is too hard.	This may take some time and effort but I'm worth it.
I can't make this any better.	It's within my power to make a difference.
I just can't do math.	I'm going to train my brain to do math.
I always make mistakes.	Miss takes help me learn.
She's so smart. I will never be the same.	I'm going to ask her how she does it!
It's good enough.	Do I care about the outcome?
Plan A didn't work, so it will never work.	Good thing the alphabet has 25 more letters!

Believe

Sometimes, as parents, we are not going to have the right answer for our child. I know… Surprise! Surprise! And think—there were generations who parented without Google! In those cases, we will need to help our child believe that we will get through the situation. A favourite expression of mine that helps me get through those times is: "This is just a moment in time and one day we will look back and laugh!"

In a workshop that we run at Parenting…With A Twist, we have a blank artist canvas that we use to illustrate this point. The blank art canvas has the foam-letter word, 'believe' in the centre of it. This symbolizes that sometimes we are not going to know the path we have to take or have the answer immediately to a question or problem we need solved. We need to have faith that once we have put it out to the Universe, acknowledged it, and stated that we are looking for some guidance in that area, we will receive help in figuring out a solution. Universe is whatever feels right for you, including substituting God for Universe.

This is a great time to teach your child to look for solutions that don't readily present themselves. I like to sum it up like this: we are all co-starring with the Universe in the movie of our lives! And that by 'believing,' you are having trust in your co-star and in yourself!

Share Stories

As much as we think kids will roll their eyes when we talk about our lives, your children do want to know what life was like for you! It humanizes you. Share your stories as a means of communicating different messages you want for your child. Give them examples of when your behaviour wasn't the best but you felt loved and then made a different choice. Give them examples of when you learned from a natural consequence, or when it took you twenty times of making a miss take to learn a valuable lesson. Also share their stories from when they were younger!

Research on family storytelling shows that when parents share more family stories with their children, these children benefit in a host of ways. For instance, experimental studies show that when parents learn to reminisce about everyday events with their preschool children in more detailed ways, their children tell richer, more complete narratives to other adults one to two years later, compared to children whose parents didn't learn the new reminiscing techniques. Children of the parents who learned new ways to reminisce also demonstrated better understanding of other people's thoughts and emotions.

These advanced narrative and emotional skills serve children well in the school years when reading complex material and learning to get along with others. In the preteen years, children whose families collaboratively discuss everyday events and family history, more often have higher self-esteem and stronger self-concepts. And adolescents with a stronger knowledge of family history have more robust identities, better coping skills, and lower rates of depression and anxiety. Family storytelling can help a child grow into a teen who feels connected to the important people in their life.

Parenting Skills Questions

Amber Highlighted Stop Sign: Use Caution When Proceeding

How do you role model this? Role modelling is a way of signalling what's appropriate in terms of how you behave, what you do, the activities you engage in, and what you believe. Remember to share these answers with your Accountability Partner!

Clapperboard: Miss Take versus Mistake & A.C.T. (Action Changes Things)

1. a) List three behaviours of your child(ren) that drive you crazy.

b) Can you see this behaviour in you or another key influencer?

c) What is a way to redirect this behaviour while you show your child, love?

d) What is this behaviour trying to tell you?

2. Think about the biggest conflict you've had with your child.

a) Can you identify which parts of the communication process you used well and which parts you didn't use at all?

b) If you were listening just to hear what they were telling you and feel where they were coming from as opposed to reacting, what was your child trying to tell you?

c) Can you bake a cake and resolve the problem?

3. How often do you engage with your child's school?

Heart: Life Experiences that Shape Us

4. a) Who are your child's cheerleaders and key influencers?

b) How often do you involve them in your child's life?

c) Could you use them to solve any current issues?

5. a) Describe a time when you let another person's opinion of your child affect your behaviour towards your child.

b) Describe a time when you let another person's opinion of you affect your behaviour towards yourself.

6. Describe a time where you've had to be your child's voice.

Circles: Different Lenses We Put On

7. a) Do you use any self-limiting words or phrases when talking with your child? If so, what changes can you make?

b) What self-limiting thoughts do you have? How are they holding you back? How can you change them?

c) What self-limiting behaviours do you engage in? How are they holding you back? What can you do instead?

8. a) What is your child's dominant personality type?

b) What is your dominant personality type?

c) Are you able to see circumstances and situations where you both fluctuate between different personality types?

d) What are your triggers?

e) What are your child's triggers?

f) Why is it easier to be happy…just because, in some situations and negative or anxious or angry in other situations?

Target: S.M.A.R.T. Goal Setting System

9. a) On average, how much time do you spend having a meaningful communication with your child?

b) On average, how much time does your child spend on media?

c) Create a S.M.A.R.T. goal with your child to change either how much time you spend having meaningful conversation with them or how much time they spend on media.

10. a) What kind of "voice" does your child have?

b) Describe a situation in which your child would be allowed to say "No" to you.

c) Describe a situation in which your child would be allowed to say "I need some time" to you.

d) Describe a situation in which your child would be allowed to say "Yes" to something you've asked them to do but then come back later and say they've changed their mind and they are now saying "No."

e) Where else can they practice the three important communication strategies shown above?

11. Choose your answers either from #8(c)(d)(f) or from #7(b)(c) and do the Elastic Band Technique to start to rewire your brain.

a) Decide if you're going to rewire your brain to not let a trigger get to you or you're going to rewire your brain to stop a specific self-limiting thought/behaviour. Write down which one you are going to work on and why you are choosing that one.

b) Get an elastic band and place it on your wrist.

c) Anytime you find you are doing what you've always done, move the elastic band to the other wrist.

d) Share this with your Accountability Partner.

(Section continued on next page.)

152

Target: S.M.A.R.T. Goal Setting System, continued

e) Share this with your child.

f) If your child is of an age where they can fully grasp what this means, invite them to participate with their own answers for #8 or #9.

g) Once you get to 22 days, decide if you feel the situation actually shifted for you, if not, check it again in another 22 days. It shouldn't take longer than 90 days!

h) CELEBRATE! You've just set yourself up for a life of success!

We are invested in your success, so please remember to connect with us

if you run into any difficulties or need any help with these questions.

**You can connect with us at our *Parenting… With A Twist*
Facebook page at Facebook.com/parentingwithatwist,
or click to parentingwithatwist.com**

"Let's raise a child that won't have to recover from their childhood."

- Pam Leo

Parenting Tip #11
I'm Not A Psychologist, I'm "Just" A Parent

Don't minimize your role as a parent by ever thinking, "I'm just a parent." Being a parent makes you a cook, alarm clock, maid, waitress, teacher, nurse, referee, handyman, security officer, photographer, counsellor, chauffeur, event planner, personal assistant, bank machine… and the list goes on. And all this for a 24/7 job with no monetary pay and no days off. This is where you give yourself a break and when you are having a bad moment, you repeat the following: "I'm not a bad parent; I am a good parent having a bad day."

My Child Is Acting Up, Please Help!
We commonly hear from parents that their children are "acting up." Even though "acting up" is described by parents differently, the underlying request is still the same: "Please help my child, my family, my sanity!"

Our process is to give the parents and children an opportunity to get everything off their minds and out of their heads onto paper. Then, our next step is to have a meeting with the whole team where we ask the following question: "Imagine our work here is complete, what would be different?" We start with the end in mind. At this point in our process, parents and children typically describe the same behaviours they want changed.

Yes! Your child does know what behaviour should change. This begs the question: Then why aren't they 'just doing it?' Well, because we aren't raising robots, and while the Nike slogan is cool, it's sometimes not that simple.

Remember the stars at the beginning, where we wanted to know what your wishes, dreams, and hopes were in being a parent? You've got through a lot of tough stuff to get to this point in the book. Let's keep going to reach those stars!

> *Children are not robots that turn on when you press a button or reboot because you press a series of buttons.*

Look In the Mirror

We have trained our kids to behave the way they do, as have the other influences in their life, be it grandparents, teachers, coaches etc. So, yes, that means you can look in the mirror and thank yourself for why your kids are the way they are! We discussed this in more detail in the the last chapter titled: "The Language of Leadership."

Why We Behave the Way We Do

In a nutshell, we all behave to get what we need/desire. Typically, we repeat behaviours if the first time we did it, it got us what we wanted. I'm your child and I need attention. I'm not getting it by asking, so I wait until you are on the phone when I know you have attention to give, and I ask for it then. How many parents have you heard complain that as soon as they get on the phone, their child needs them for something? I have also learned that if it's something I want and there is a high probability that you will say "No," then the chances of me asking while you are on the phone become that much greater. Why? Because, in your distracted state, there is a higher chance you will say "Yes." Kids are super smart and more than likely know us better than we know ourselves!

Consequences To Our Behaviour

Every behaviour has a meaning and a consequence. I choose to wear a blue shirt and the consequence is that I get a compliment on my eyes that day. I choose to wear a white shirt and eat spaghetti and the consequence is that I get a stain on my shirt.

Meeting My Needs

Based on that consequence and if I got my need/desire met, I may repeat that behaviour again. In the example above with the phone call: if I got my need met for attention and then got a further desire met by a "Yes" to something I wanted, then I would more than likely ask you something again when I know you are distracted. If I got a compliment when wearing a blue shirt, I would more than likely wear that shirt again and/or be attracted to more clothes or accessories in that colour. I may choose not to wear white again thinking that I'll stain it.

Iceberg Behaviour Analogy

While we only see the behaviour that the person is displaying, we often forget that what is being displayed is really indicative of how they are feeling or how they have learned to get a need met in the past. Think of this like an iceberg—typically you only see the tip of the iceberg sticking out. This is akin to the behaviour someone is displaying. The layers underneath the iceberg you don't see are akin to the reasons why a person is acting that way.

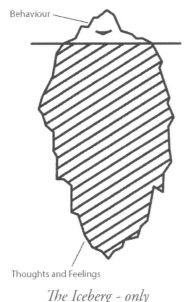

Behaviour

Thoughts and Feelings

The Iceberg - only the tip shows!

If it's your child, you are going to want to take the time to investigate the reasons. So instead of judging or reacting to that behaviour, we need to simply (ha! ha!) remind ourselves that the behaviour is just that: someone trying to have a need met. It's your job to figure out what the behaviour is telling you they need!

Seeing Lying As A Form Of Problem Solving

It's important to mention lying in this section as I'd like parents to reframe the way they think of lying. Most think of it as a moral issue and take it personally. We often get parents who are appalled that their children lied to them. Remember, that is just the behaviour we are seeing, just the tip of the iceberg. It's our job to investigate why they are lying. So if it's not a moral issue, what is it? It's a problem–solving issue, a lack of skill issue, and an avoiding consequence issue. Our children often know right from wrong; could it be that's why they are lying? They don't want to get in trouble for what they've done and they're using lying to solve their problems. What that means is that they need to learn different problem-solving skills. As a parent, instead of judging or reacting to the lie, help them work on their ability to problem solve.

Here is a funny story to illustrate how lying is really just a method of problem solving, not a moral issue. I went to pick up my son from a play date. When I arrived, the mother said that she didn't realize that my son was allergic to anything, but she was glad he had let her know. Due to his allergies, she had made him a grilled cheese sandwich for dinner as opposed to the spinach pasta they were having. Well, I was a little speechless because I knew he didn't have any food allergies. I didn't want to embarrass him in front of his friend and her mom, so instead, we talked about this untruth on the way home.

Pros & Cons Of A Situation

My son knew that if he said he had allergies he wouldn't be encouraged to try something new and could get something entirely different made for him. Smart boy! While I didn't want to discourage him from thinking outside the box when problem solving, I also needed him to know that telling a lie wasn't okay either. We discussed what else he could have said or done in the situation and the pros and cons of each alternative statement or action.

-He could have said that he didn't like spinach.
(Pro: being honest; Con: they may have said, eat it anyway)

-He could have said that he wasn't hungry.
(Pro: wouldn't have to eat food he didn't like; Con: he'd be hungry)

-He could have said that he decided to go home for dinner.
(Pro: wouldn't have to eat food he didn't like; Con: may not be invited for dinner again)

-He could have said that in our house when we don't like something that is for dinner, it's our responsibility to make something else. The alternative has to be simple and any mess cleaned up by the person who made it. And he could have asked to do that.
(Pro: being honest; Con: may have said that's not our rule and may have had to eat it anyway)

-He could have eaten it and spit it into his napkin.
(Pro: wouldn't have to eat food he didn't like; Con: he'd be hungry and they might catch him)

-He could have fed it to the dog discreetly.
(Pro: wouldn't have to eat food he didn't like; Con: he'd be hungry, they might catch him and the dog might get sick)

We came up with a plan for him to talk to his friend and her mom about his untruth and his reasoning behind why he did it. He could ask her what he could do if this was to happen again to see what her house rules were about not liking the dinner that is being served. Great life skill to give your child: talk the problem out and come up with solutions!

No Forced Sorry

Don't force a child to say sorry. Have a conversation with your child to help them come to the understanding of why their behaviour was inappropriate and what they need to do to show the person that they are sorry. Sometimes this isn't automatic or immediate. Yes, because they are not a robot!

You are raising a child, not programming a robot.

If we force our child to say sorry we miss out on so much. In the situation above, I would have missed out on understanding his 'why' and him feeling heard. He would have missed understanding that there are many ways to solve a problem, that it's important to think through a decision, and that one should look at the positive and negative in each potential choice.

Children's Behaviours Must Serve Them

You need to look at the behaviours that you reward in your children and ask yourself the question: Are these behaviours that will serve them well in life? If not, you will need to start redirecting that behaviour. If so, then continue to reward them for it as you are helping them form healthy habits for life.

A further question you need to ask yourself is: if others are displaying behaviours to get needs met, might you perhaps be doing the same thing? Of course, we all do! Be aware—your child will mirror your behaviour of how you get your needs met. Also, somebody might judge you inaccurately because only the tip of your 'iceberg' is sticking out. While you may know why you are acting a certain way, others may not.

An example of this would be if you are having a bad day at work. You come home and find out that your child forgot to turn the dishwasher on and you react negatively. If you could admit to them that you weren't really that upset about the dishwasher but more upset about what happened at work, you could use this situation to help your child understand the iceberg analogy. Then you could brainstorm with your child about what you could do differently moving forward, to get work frustration out as opposed to taking it out on your child. Your child will see that while you got a need met (the need to let out frustration) you didn't do it in the healthiest way (taking it out on your child.) An idea that could come up while you are brainstorming, is that in future, you could go for a walk as soon as you get home.

Your Child's Needs Are What Get Them In the Most Trouble

It is super important to start helping your child figure out what their needs are. If one of their needs is deemed as selfish, it will still need to get met. If the other members of the house would consider it selfish if you went for walk when you get home from work, instead of doing the multitude of things that a working parent could do when they get home, you would want to set the example that being selfish was what was necessary for your mental health. Your children need to see this modelled by you so that they don't turn into adults that think taking care of themselves is a negative attribute.

Being selfish was not encouraged in my household growing up. Selfish was a bad word and you didn't want anybody suggesting you were selfish. I've since realized that being 'selfish' is actually quite acceptable. If you are not meeting your own needs, then your needs might not be met. Examine this in your life: what needs are you putting on others to meet for you? As a baby, you are not perceived as selfish when you make your needs known. Why should we not all be that keenly aware of what we need in the moment and ask for it? What needs do your child have that they 'act out' to get met? To figure this out, look at the behaviour that gets your child in the most trouble. Because it's so important our needs are met, we will act out to get them met. Your job is to teach your children to identify their needs and how to ask for help to get them met, or meet it themselves in a healthy way.

> *Look at the behaviour that gets your child in the most trouble as the way to identify their biggest need, and then help them to meet that need in a healthier way.*

Selfish & Entitled

We defined in another chapter the difference between privilege and entitlement. I'd like to explore the difference between being selfish and feeling entitled. As I've highlighted above, being selfish really is quite healthy; however, feeling entitled is unhealthy. In my experience in dealing with people who feel entitled, they erase their need to take responsibility for their life. Everything is always another person's fault.

When one feels entitled to get whatever they want, whenever they want it, there is no need to plan to reach their goals. So, when something doesn't work out, there isn't any learning about what they could do differently next time. There are no miss takes in their lives! Such a mentality can actually be destructive to their life, and those around them. Be aware of the difference between selfish and titled for both yourself and your children!

The Simplicity of Life

Life is really that simple:

1. We have a need/desire.

2. We act a certain way to have this need/desire met.

3. There is a consequence to this action.

4. Depending on the consequence and whether it met this need/desire, we will continue to do that same action in the future, or we will adapt our behaviour until our need/desire is met.

5. Whoever is around us the most shapes our behaviour and acts as our mirror to what behaviours we model.

We talked about behaviours having consequences, and based on these consequences, the behaviour may or may not be repeated, dependent upon reaching the desired goal. It's important to not rise to the negativity with any sort of reaction, as that will feed into a child behaving in a way that won't get the behaviour we want.

The good news is that you don't need to be a child psychologist or a math teacher to help your child. The even better news is that with understanding the iceberg analogy, and just how simple life is, you can help your child. We used common parent concerns to illustrate this and invite you to use this understanding with other issues you may be having.

Parenting Skills Questions

Amber Highlighted Stop Sign: Use Caution When Proceeding

How do you role model this? Role modelling is a way of signalling what's appropriate in terms of how you behave, what you do, the activities you engage in, and what you believe. Remember to share these answers with your Accountability Partner!

Circles: Different Lenses We Put On

1. a) What could the different titles of your child's movie be if they were based on the single points in time where they had made a miss take?

b) What could the different titles of your child's movie be if they were based on their life as a journey (as opposed to a single moment in time)?

c) Which title are you going to choose to focus on?

2. a) What could the different titles of your movie be if they were based on the single points in time where you had made a miss take?

b) What could the different titles of your movie be if they were based on your life as a journey (as opposed to a single moment in time)?

c) Which title are you going to choose to focus on?

3. a) How do you view miss takes that happen on a path to success?

b) How can you embrace miss takes that happen on a path to success for both yourself and your child?

4. The next time you think your child should 'just do it,' are you open to the fact that you are not raising robots but children who will need your guidance, patience and love to get there?

5. a) Define what selfish means to you.

b) Do you need to shift this definition?

c) What everyday indulgence could you take for yourself, to show your child that it's okay to put your needs first?

Heart: Life Experiences that Shape Us

6. a) Select a situation where your child has lied to you.

b) See if you can figure out why they lied. In other words, what was the underlying problem that they were trying to solve by telling a lie?

c) What is a different way you could help them solve this problem?

7. What story could you use from your life to share the iceberg analogy with your child?

Clapperboard: Miss Take versus Mistake & A.C.T. (Action Changes Things)

8. a) What are your child's top three needs/desires? How do you know this?

b) How are these needs/desires met?

c) Can you see any ways that you could help them meet those needs/desires in a healthy way?

Target: S.M.A.R.T. Goal Setting System

9. Create a S.M.A.R.T. goal for how to shift your answer from 1.(c), 2.(c), 3 (b), 4 or 5(c).

We are invested in your success, so please remember to connect with us

if you run into any difficulties or need any help with these questions.

**You can connect with us at our *Parenting... With A Twist*
Facebook page at Facebook.com/parentingwithatwist,
or click to parentingwithatwist.com**

"Who you are speaks so loudly, I can't hear what you are saying."

\- Ralph Waldo Emerson

Parenting Tip #12
Children Learn What They Live

Role Modeling

Role modeling is a way of signalling what's appropriate in terms of how you behave, what you do, the activities you engage in and what you believe.

Are you hopeful, engaged, thriving, self-sufficient, and prosperous? In other words, are you a role model of what it means to be Success-Ready?!

As Freud said, the definition of insanity is to do the same thing over and over and expect different results. Look in your notebook and see where you can shift. Start by breaking the cycles you've learned or adopted over the years.

Three Key Pieces Of Being A Successful Role Model

There are three key pieces to consider in role modelling:

#1: Do you have the knowledge and ability to teach your child to be success-ready?

#2: Are you the walking definition of what it means to be success-ready?

#3: How do you deal with the obstacles life throws at you?

All the role-model questions in each chapter helped us to see that it comes down to YOU! If you don't know how to give these things to yourself, how are you going to know how to teach your child to do so?

Put On Your Air Mask First

Think of the safety speech you get when a plane takes off. You must put your air mask on first before you put on your children's, otherwise you may not be around to help them.

You Control Your Destiny

In life, sometimes you start out with a map, directions, a sign that tells you where you are going, and, if you don't take the direct route, what to expect. Sometimes you stay the course and finish in exactly the designated time. Other times, you don't. Perhaps there is no sign to tell you how long you should take to get there or what might happen if you take another path. What comes into play when an obstacle presents itself? Basically, it will come down to your habits, behaviours, and everyday choices.

When Life Throws You Lemons

Okay…so you are proceeding down your path of life and you hit an obstacle. Do you stop? Do you turn around? Do you ask for help? Do you give up? Do you say, "I can't"? Do you regroup? Do you think of solutions? What do you do when life throws you a curve ball?

And, like many obstacles that you face in life, you have a choice as to your attitude. I personally do my very best to take obstacles in stride and keep a positive outlook (except, of course, when I don't). Note though, that although you might be embracing this obstacle whole heartedly, your physical body can still take on certain stresses. So it is very important to maintain a healthy body as well!

Sometimes the path ahead may seem long but you might be able to see markers along the way and know clearly what is next. This makes some people feel very comfortable. They enjoy having things in a particular order and clarity. If that is you, what do you do when that changes? What do you do to ensure your life runs like that?

How about when the path doesn't seem as clear? What about if it's not marked? What if there appears to be another obstacle? What if you've done the path before and you know what to anticipate?

What if you have seemingly identical choices? What if you've prioritized one higher than the other? What if somebody else in your life has prioritized one higher than the other? Which one do you choose? How much choice do you actually have, depending on who the person is who has potentially prioritized it for you?

What if you are being forced into a certain direction? What if you feel closed in? What if you enjoy being forced into a decision? What if somebody is standing in the way of your seemingly only path?

What if you have a choice of paths: one marked, one not marked? What if they look as though they are going in the same direction? What if you have people who tell you to only take the marked path? Who do you listen to? How do you make your choice? Who says which choice is dangerous? Which choice is safe?

Learn To F.L.Y. (First Love Yourself)

We would love to help you Learn To F.L.Y. (First Love Yourself) as a parent so that you can help your children. Remember that love is a verb, which means it requires action. Take action today to get super clear on your values around time, money and expectations. Begin to learn the life skills to make yourself success-ready. How awesome will it feel to confidently show your children what success-ready looks and feels like?

Please connect with us if Learn To F.L.Y. resonates with you, as we can help you get to the next level. (Our contact information can be found at the end of each chapter in the "Parenting Skills Question" section.)

Parenting Skills Questions

Dig out your answers from the very first Parenting Skills Questions that you did at the beginning of the book in the chapter titled: "Ready! Set! Go!"

Star: Hopes, Wishes, Dreams & Desires

1. Of the dreams, wishes, hopes, and desires as a parent that you wrote down as 'stars,' from our very first exercise together,

a) which did you reach?

b) which did you not reach?

Circles: Different Lenses We Put On

2. How has your 'parenting lens' shifted?

Clapperboard: Miss Take versus Mistake & A.C.T. (Action Changes Things)

3. a) What actions have you taken to make your 'parenting stars' come true?

b) What actions do you still need to take?

4. What renewed passion do you feel for being a parent?

5. What new habits have you developed that will help you be the parent you've always wanted to be?

Heart: Life Experiences that Shape Us

6. You get to create the parent you want to be. What are you planning your future relationship with your child to be like, based on the work you are doing?

Amber Highlighted Stop Sign: Use Caution When Proceeding

7. In knowing that you are shaping the type of parent your child is going to be, is there anything else you need to work through?

Happy Face: Happy…Just Because

8. With the full awareness that no matter what you do, you are going to get a bad review from your child at some point, can you be happy…just because?

Target: S.M.A.R.T. Goal Setting System

9. Of the dreams, wishes, hopes, and desires as a parent that you wrote down as 'star,' from our very first exercise together—the *Ready! Set! GO!* Questions:

a) For the 'stars' you reached, what habits and mindsets helped you accomplish this? Share these results with your child!

b) For the 'stars' you didn't reach, what got in your way? Reach out to your Accountability Partner or us if you need help to figure this out.

c) Write a S.M.A.R.T. goal to reach the 'stars' you haven't yet reached. Share it with your Accountability Partner and us.

10. Check your S.M.A.R.T. goal for completing this book from the very first exercise we did together: the *Ready! Set! GO!* Questions:

a) Did you reach your target completion date?

b) If you reached your completion date, what habits and mindsets helped you accomplish this?

c) If you didn't reach your completion date, what got in your way? Reach out to your Accountability Partner or us if you need help to figure this out.

d) Write a S.M.A.R.T. goal to reach the 'stars' you haven't yet reached. Share it with your Accountability Partner and us.

e) Celebrate as you read to the end of the book!

We are invested in your success, so please remember to connect with us

if you run into any difficulties or need any help with these questions.

You can connect with us at our *Parenting… With A Twist*
Facebook page at Facebook.com/parentingwithatwist,
or click to parentingwithatwist.com

Certificate

Here at *Parenting... With A Twist*, we're so proud of your commitment to your children that we want to recognize your awesomeness with this certificate. Tear this out of the book and put it on your wall!

If you'd like to download a free colour copy, just visit us at ParentingWithATwist.com and look for the link.

Congratulations! Your decision makes a difference for your family, and for our future world.

CERTIFICATE OF
Awesomeness

Proudly Presented to: _____

**For Committing to Raising Confident
and Success-Ready Children**

Presented by: _____

PARENTING
...WITH A *Twist*

Reference Material

Achor, S. (2012, January-February) Positive Intelligence [critique of studies] Retrieved from https://hbr.org/2012/01/positive-intelligence

Barrow, B. (2006, 19 July) 19 minutes - how long working parents give their children [analysis of statistics] Retrieved from: http://www.dailymail.co.uk/news/article-396609/19-minutes--long-working-parents-children.html

Bayless, K. (n.d.) What is Helicopter Parenting? [article] Retrieved from: http://www.parents.com/parenting/better-parenting/what-is-helicopter-parenting/

Berman, R. (2015, November 4) His students were struggling, so he 'flipped' his classroom. Then everything changed. [article] Retrieved from http://www.upworthy.com/his-students-were-struggling-so-he-flipped-his-classroom-then-everything-changed

Bryan, B. (2016, May 24) More Millennials are living with their parents than at any other time in American history [article] https://www.sott.net/article/318993-More-millennials-are-living-with-their-parents-than-at-any-other-time-in-American-history

Conference Board of Canada. (n.d.) Employability Skills 2000+ [Summation of findings] Retrieved from http://www.conferenceboard.ca/topics/education/learning-tools/employability-skills.aspx

Davidson, C. (2011, Sept 23) Standardized tests for everyone? In the Internet age, that's the wrong answer. [article] Retrieved from https://www.washingtonpost.com/opinions/standardized-tests-for-everyone-in-the-internet-age-thats-the-wrong-answer/2011/09/21/gIQA7SZwqK_story.html?utm_term=.f64d4bca3361

Denee, R. (n.d.) Minute-to-minute Living. [statistics analyzed] Retrieved from https://realtruth.org/articles/120128-001.html

Duke, MP, Lazarus A, & Fivush R. (2008, June) Knowledge of family history as a clinically useful index of psychological well-being and prognosis: A brief report. [statistical report] Retrieved from http://www.ncbi.nlm.nih.gov/pubmed/22122420

Everfi. (2016, April 1) New survey finds that more parents are talking to their kids about money, but lack knowledge on important topics. [survey results] Retrieved from http://everfi.com/finlitmonthsurvey/

Gillett, R. (2015, July 23) Research says this is what you need to teach your kids in kindergarten if you ever want them to go to college or get a job. [article] Retrieved from http://www.businessinsider.com/future-success-could-be-determined-early-2015-7#ixzz3hCRlz0Oc

Gillett, R. & Baer, D. (2016, May 6) Science says parents of successful kids have these 13 things in common. [synthesis of multiple studies] Retrieved from http://www.techinsider.io/how-parents-set-their-kids-up-for-success-2016-4?pundits_only=0&get_all_comments=1&no_reply_filter=1

Grimsley, S. (n.d.) Pygmalion Effect: Definition & Examples [lesson plan] Retrieved from http://study.com/academy/lesson/pygmalion-effect-definition-examples-quiz.html

Hango, D. (2011) Delaying Post-secondary Education: Who Delays and for How Long? Retrieved from http://www.statcan.gc.ca/pub/81-595-m/81-595-m2011090-eng.pdf

Hu, J & Liden, R. (2013, December) Making a Difference in the Teamwork: Linking Team Prosocial Motivation to Team Processes and Effectiveness [study] Retrieved from: https://www.researchgate.net/journal/0001-4273_The_Academy_of_Management_Journal

Kyriacou, M. (2015, April 1) Ditch the mummy guilt: Study shows amount of time spent with kids isn't crucial to their success. Retrieved from http://www.mindfood.com/article/ditch-the-mummy-guilt-study-shows-amount-of-time-spent-with-kids-isnt-crucial-to-their-success/

Larson, K., Russ, S, Bergen B., Nelson, Olson, L. & Halfon, N. (2015, February) Cognitive Ability at Kindergarten Entry and Socioeconomic Status. [summary of research studies] Retrieved from http://pediatrics.aappublications.org/content/pediatrics/135/2/e440.full.pdf

Lopex, S. (2014, April 10) Not Enough Students Are Success-Ready [article] Retrieved from http://www.gallup.com/businessjournal/168242/not-enough-students-success-ready.aspx

Lyubomirsky, S, King, L & Diener, E. U (2005) The Benefits of Frequent Positive Affect: Does Happiness Lead to Success? Retrieved from http://www.apa.org/pubs/journals/releases/bul-1316803.pdf

Malcolm H. (2012, April 24) Millennials struggle with financial literacy [article] Retrieved from http://usatoday30.usatoday.com/money/perfi/basics/story/2012-04-23/millenials-financial-knowledge/54494856/1

Mastergeorge, A. et al (2013) Positive Parent-Child Relation- ships —Beginning with the transition to parent-hood, parents and families develop warm relationships that nurture their child's learning and development. [study findings] Retrieved from http://eclkc.ohs.acf.hhs.gov/hslc/tta-system/family/docs/parent-child-relationships.pdf

Mendoza, M & Liedtk, M. (2015, January) How Google Is Embracing Team Work And Workplace Wellness—The tech giant released new research on Tuesday about building productive and cohesive teams. [article] Retrieved from http://www.huffingtonpost.com/entry/how-google-is-embracing-team-work-and-workplace-wellness_us_564c925ae4b045bf3df1d032?nzj5g66r=

Mikler, V. (2015, Dec 5) Iceberg Model: Using Motivation to Enhance Performance [research oriented blog] Retrieved from http://instituteod.com/news.php?id=181&cat_id=&p=2&search=

Milkie, Melissa A, Kei M. Nomaguchi and Kathleen E. Denny. (2014) How Does the Amount of Time Mothers Spend with Children and Adolescents Matter? Retrieved from https://socy.umd.edu/publication/forthcoming-milkie-melissa-kei-m-nomaguchi-and-kathleen-e-denny-"how-does-amount-time

Money Habits. (n.d.) The Rule of Thirds [blog post] Retrieved from http://www.moneyhabits.com/rule_of_thirds.htm

National Education Association (n.d.) Research Spotlight on Homework: NEA Reviews of the Research on Best Practices in Education. Retrieved from http://www.nea.org/tools/16938.htm

NCES. (n.d.) Average length of school year and average length of school day, by selected characteristics. [survey results] Retrieved from http://nces.ed.gov/surveys/pss/tables/table_15.asp

Peck, E. (2015) Google Has Discovered The 5 Key Traits Employees Need To Succeed—An Ivy League degree isn't as important as trust, for starters. [article] Retrieved from http://www.huffingtonpost.com/entry/google-employee-success-traits_us_564cd621e4b031745cef50fe

PRB — Population Reference Bureau (2015, April) Time With Parents Key for Adolescents [analysis] Retrieved from http://www.prb.org/Publications/Articles/2015/parental-time.aspx

Reese, E. (2013, Dec 9) What Kids Learn From Hearing Family Stories: Reading to children has education benefits, of course, but so does sharing tales from the past. [presenting research findings] Retrieved from http://www.theatlantic.com/education/archive/2013/12/what-kids-learn-from-hearing-family-stories/282075/

Robinson, Jacqueline. (2000, Sept 15) What Are Employability Skills? Retrieved from: http://www.foretica.org/wp-content/uploads/2016/01/employability-skills.pdf

Schulte, B. (2015, March 28) Making time for kids? Study says quality trumps quantity. [article]

Retrieved from https://www.washingtonpost.com/local/making-time-for-kids-study-says-quality-trumps-quantity/2015/03/28/10813192-d378-11e4-8fce-3941fc548f1c_story.html

University of Phoenix. (2014, February 25) Homework anxiety: Survey reveals how much homework K-12 students are assigned and why teachers deem it beneficial. [article]

http://www.phoenix.edu/news/releases/2014/02/survey-reveals-how-much-homework-k-12-students-are-assigned-why-teachers-deem-it-beneficial.html

Zenger, J. & Folkman, J. (2013, March 15) The Ideal Praise-to-Criticism Ratio. [article] Retrieved from: https://hbr.org/2013/03/the-ideal-praise-to-criticism

About the Author

AMBER SCOTCHBURN is an internationally-recognized parenting expert, and the co-author of the bestselling book *Dynamo Diaries: Success Secrets of 21 Shining Stars*. She is the founder of Amber Scotchburn Training Consultants, a life skills-based training company.

Social worker, teacher, tutoring agency CEO, bestselling author, and nationally sought-after parenting expert, Amber Scotchburn finally provides what the everyday parent is looking for: a manual full of parenting tips to help YOU be the parent you've always wanted to be.

The everyday parent includes co-parents, single parents, step-parents (or, as Amber likes to call them, Bonus Parents), dads, moms, new parents... and the list goes on!

As an everyday parent, you will be able to do your own Parenting Skills Assessment through reading this book. And then, place your trust in Amber's Signature *Success...With A Twist System* to help you transform the knowledge gleaned from this skills assessment to empower you to discover the positive parent within!

Instead of using punitive measures as your first line of discipline, let's discover the magic in getting to know your child and fall back in love with them at every age. Let's learn why it's important for your child to say "no" and even lie to you. Let's explore not allowing school grades to define your child. Let's understand all of your child's behaviours, especially the ones that drive you the most insane!

Parenting...With A Twist will keep you reading more, as Amber's passion for people, encouraging story-telling, love of humour, uncanny insights, and her interactive process of teaching comes through on every single page.

Index

179

Made in the USA
Charleston, SC
31 December 2016